Prayer PathWay is original in its conception and brilliantly structured—and it does just what it promises! This beautiful book rides on the vast sea of God's Word and draws its life from its depths. The wisdom of the praying saints of the centuries provides inspirational sidebars that are a joy to read in themselves. Here is a volume that will ignite the prayers and fire the devotion of every reader/sojourner. There is nothing quite like *Prayer PathWay*.

> —**R. Kent Hughes**, Senior Pastor Emeritus, College Church, Wheaton; Visiting Professor, Practical Theology, Westminster Theological Seminary, Philadelphia

Prayer is a profound privilege and yet such a mystery. Kathi will help you to learn to pray in such a way as to appreciate both. Her acrostic provides a helpful, insightful concept, and the historical quotes about prayer are a great addition to the book.

> —**Susan Hunt**, Author, *Prayers of the Bible*; former Director of Women's Ministries, Presbyterian Church in America

Kathi Westlund has given the church the fruit of twenty years of prayer labor. Forged in the realities of everyday life, this journal is not an academic treatise on prayer; it is a peek into the lessons learned by a seasoned prayer-warrior. Kathi has refined her understanding of prayer through countless prayer burdens, and this has given us a powerful tool to bring us into a deeper relationship with God and a deeper joy in participating in His work in this world. Through instruction, encouragement, and admonition, *Prayer PathWay* is a guide to lead us to the throne of grace, focus our prayers, and challenge our hearts. Laden with Scripture, this volume is inspirational, educational, and intensely practical. What might God do through the prayers of His people fueled by this extensive guide? I highly commend this outstanding resource to you as you consider your part in the great work and blessing of prayer.

> —**Sally Michael**, Cofounder, Children Desiring God; Author, *God's Names*

Prayer PathWay will help you to organize your prayer life. Its purpose is that simple. But it's more than just a prayer organizer. This tool is also the fruit of countless hours both in prayer and thinking about prayer by Kathi Westlund. Some may find her pathway too structured for their personality; others will find it orderly and clarifying. Some may hesitate at a few of the sources of the inspirational quotations in the margins; others will happily glean what they can from them. But every Christian can benefit from the Scriptures the author has collected for each topic, as well as the suggestions of how to pray for others, such as one's spouse. In short, there's something here for just about every Christian looking for help in prayer.

 —**Donald S. Whitney**, Professor of Biblical Spirituality, The Southern Baptist Theological Seminary; Author, *Praying the Bible*

Prayer PATHWAY

Prayer PATHWAY

Journeying in a Life of Prayer

KATHI LAMBRIDES WESTLUND

P U B L I S H I N G

P.O. BOX 817 • PHILLIPSBURG • NEW JERSEY 08865-0817

Additional, printable forms and instructions for creating a customizable Prayer PathWay notebook are available at www.prpbooks.com and www.prayerpathway.com.

For
Gabriella, Abraham,
Salem, Samuel, and Jacob

God gave you to us to teach us how to pray.

Our day begins with prayer:
Christ be beside me; Christ be before me;
Christ be behind me; King of my heart.
Christ be within me; Christ be below me;
Christ be above me, Never to part.

Our day ends with prayer:
Good-night! Good-night!
Far flies the light;
But still God's love
Shall flame above,
Making all bright.
Good-night! Good-night!

And in between: more prayer with you and for you . . .

"For this child I [have] prayed."
1 Samuel 1:27

Christ is the path and
Christ the prize.

JOHN S. B. MONSELL

CONTENTS

PART 1

PREPARATIONS

INTRODUCTION

WE ARE SOJOURNERS IN THIS LIFE. Each day, we travel an unfamiliar path toward a sure destination. God is our ever-present companion—guiding and protecting, comforting and convicting us, but we are often unaware of Him.

Prayer is our means of acknowledging God's presence and seeking His help on our daily journey. It is God's way of giving us access to Him. He commands us to pray because He knows that we need Him. We need His redemption, His guidance, His courage, His forgiveness, His sustenance, His peace. He knows that we need what He has—that we have no where else to turn! C. S. Lewis expressed it: "To what will you look for help if you will not look to that which is stronger than yourself?" Simon Peter admitted it: "Lord, to whom shall we go? You have the words of eternal life" (John 6:68). And God Himself says: "Call to me and I will answer you, and will tell me great and hidden things that you have not known" (Jeremiah 33:3).

In heeding God's command to pray, we become part of a humbling and powerful collaboration:

- *God* hears us and answers us. (Jeremiah 33:3)
- *Jesus* prays for us. (Romans 8:34)
- The *Holy Spirit* helps us pray. (Romans 8:26)

My steps have held fast to your paths; my feet have not slipped. I call upon you, for you will answer me, O God; incline your ear to me; hear my words.

PSALM 17:5–6

II

prayer we:

praise God with the adoration and respect that only a King deserves.
- run to our Judge for the relief of **repenting** and the **resolve** to obey.
- **ask** the Father for things only His children dare ask.
- **yield** to His greater wisdom and mysterious providences.
- **give thanks** to the Giver for His unmerited goodness to us.
- find **refuge** and **rejoice** in the fact that the Almighty God has heard us.
- take rest in His peace: the great *shalom*.

MY PATH

The method of prayer, Prayer PathWay, found in this book is one result of more than thirty years of my own prayer journey. As I walked life's path of joy and pain, I longed for a guide that would help me to pray when I couldn't find refrains to reflect my happiness or laments to echo my sorrow. So I read book after book after book searching for prayer guidance. But it was all there in my own Bible: words breathed by God, through men; words that have strengthened and awed God's people throughout the centuries since Christ walked His own earthly path of joy and pain toward the cross. As I opened my eyes to behold the wonders in the Word, I was strengthened for the journey. And my desire for the Word was ignited by seeing what God had for me there.

Open my eyes, that I may behold wondrous things out of your law. I am a sojourner on the earth; hide not your commandments from me!

PSALM 119:18–19

As I started using my Bible as a prayer book, I saw a path of prayer emerge. I saw that God's people were praising, repenting, asking, yielding, thanking, and rejoicing—over and over, in all situations, through all generations.

In my other reading, I saw that since Bible times God's wise ones have attempted to put their journeys into words. Those words have left a trail to strengthen the hearts and fuel the prayers of subsequent sojourners like me. I saw the timeless truth of the Bible underscored but not replaced, echoing down the centuries—pointing me to Christ.

Using the Bible in prayer gave me a prayer voice that was more sure and settled than my own. I began to tread a path of prayer that has helped me to pray through my days.

I was able to rejoice in hope, to be patient in trials, to be constant in prayer, humbled by the knowledge that Jesus walked this way before and encouraged by the fact that He walks with me now!

GOD IS CALLING US TO PRAY

Lead thou me on.
The night is dark,
and I am far from home,
Lead thou me on.
Keep thou my feet;
I do not ask to see
the distant scene;
one step enough for me.

JOHN HENRY
NEWMAN

When God calls us to pray, He isn't calling us to do something *for* Him. He's calling us to receive something *from* Him—something we need: His light for our daily journey.

God knows that we need His light for the uncertain terrain we encounter every day. He has promised: "I will turn the darkness before them into light, the rough places into level ground . . ." (Isaiah 42:16b).

The Bible is rich with the imagery of walking and of light. We moderns have a hard time appreciating what it would be like to have our feet be our main mode of transport—we use fast cars on smooth highways. And we can't imagine navigating in the dark—we flick a switch to flood our surroundings in light. Imagine walking at night on a rocky trail. The flickering light from a lantern doesn't reveal much of the path, just enough for the next few steps. Truthfully, if we knew what was ahead of us on the path, we might be too frightened to go on! God shows us just enough.

The psalmist said: "Your word is a lamp to my feet and a light to my path" (Psalm 119:105). God has the light we need. We can't create light for our path by rubbing sticks together! But God has provided a steady light through His Word.

Jesus is the Word of God in human form (John 1:1–18). He was sent "to give light to those who sit in darkness . . . to guide our feet into the way of peace" (Luke 1:79). He said of Himself: "I am the light of the world. Whoever follows me will not walk in darkness, but will have the light of life" (John 8:12). With Jesus we walk in light.

God has given us the Holy Spirit as our much-needed teacher. He said: "I will put my Spirit within you, and cause you to walk in my statutes and be careful to obey my rules" (Ezekiel 36:27). Again, the walking motif! We are enabled to walk in the truth because of the guidance of the

Helper: "When the Spirit of truth comes, he will guide you into all the truth" (John 16:13).

We, sojourners, have Jesus as our light and the Holy Spirit as our guide as we seek to "walk humbly with [our] God" (Micah 6:8). We are not traveling alone. The presence and the power of the Triune God are ours.

THE BEAUTY OF A WELL-WORN PATH

We've all had the experience of carefully relying on a map or GPS to navigate a complicated route to a new place. Then, gradually, with repeated trips on the same road, we don't need to rely on navigational tools. We have internalized the map. It has become part of us. We know the way.

The same thing happens with prayer.

This guide is not meant to be a formula but a pattern—not a chain but a path—to help you as you make your way. God uses well-established spiritual disciplines to guide us when our emotions run thin and our motivations are weak. Every Christian is prayerless in some, perhaps many, seasons of life. Like any frequently traveled path, a path of prayer allows our faltering steps to progress, even if our hearts are not fully engaged. Often, the heart is sparked by the comforting routine of prayer, courage is restored, joy eventually returns.

We are all, gradually, moving toward hard times in life, if we haven't gone through them already. You won't learn to pray in the emergency room—that's where you'll speechlessly lean into Jesus. You won't learn to pray in your overturned car—that's where you'll just cry out His name. You won't learn to pray in your living room while reeling from a loved one's bad decisions—that's when you'll just weep to God. Learning the way when life is somewhat stable makes us familiar with the path so that we can run straight to Him in the dark, like a nightmare-scared child instinctively making his way to his parents' bed.

We are with God all the way; He is the route, and He is the destination.

Just because your heart is cold and prayerless, get you into the presence of the loving Father.... Just tell Him how sinful and cold and dark all is: it is the Father's loving heart will give light and warmth to yours.

ANDREW MURRAY

THE GUIDE

A Brief Overview

PRAYER PATHWAY is a tool designed to help you pray through your days and through your life. It can be used in many different ways as your prayer needs change. I give some suggestions in the next section and in "Prayer Planning" on page 243.

The heart of this book is PRAYERS, an acrostic for seven areas of prayer (Praise, Repent, Ask, Yield, Express thanks, Rejoice, Shalom). Each section is a portion of a daily prayer journey with Bible passages to guide your praying and inspiring quotes to encourage you with the thoughts of sages who have traveled this way before you. There is an extra page at the end of each section for you to record additional verses, quotations, and notes.

This Christian way whereon I walk is no untried and uncharted road, but a road beaten hard by the footsteps of saints, apostles, prophets, and martyrs.

JOHN BAILLIE

Proceed through the sections, praying. Linger as your heart requires or hurry as your schedule dictates. Or you may turn right to the section you know you need and pray there. You might use sticky tabs to mark your stopping place in each section. Please don't allow yourself to get trapped in rigid routines! Following a form doesn't please God. He wants us to come to Him to be unburdened

(Matthew 11:28–30) not to be crushed by greater burdens (Matthew 23:4–12). Conversely, don't confuse
spiritual discipline with legalism. Developing strong
patterns of spiritual disciplines when our hearts are
inclined helps us to press on when our hearts are not.

In every journey
there must be a
first step.

J. C. RYLE

My experience has also shown that ingrained habits of prayer serve as a
beacon when my to-do list threatens to snuff out my prayer time.

Many people find their prayer lives are more focused and disciplined
when they have prayer lists and schedules. Also, having a record of God's
past faithfulnesses to look back on can do much to bolster faith in Him.
So as well as the seven prayer sections, I've provided some forms and
resources:

- Prayer Themes: Prayer guides with daily themes for praying for your
  spouse, your children, or other loved ones.
- Prayer Plan: Reproducible forms for creating a weekly prayer planner
  and prayer lists for each day of the week.
- Index of Quotations: An alphabetized list of those quoted within
  this book, along with the source and any notes or comments. I've
  marked my favorite sources (recommended reading) with ❦.

You may want to fill out the forms right in this book, or you may prefer to print them out to create your own customizable prayer notebook.

THE MAP

A Suggested Itinerary

PRAYERS

*Start with **Praise**,* because: "Great is the LORD, and greatly to be praised!" (1 Chronicles 16:25a). Read a passage or a quote. If it expresses your heart, pray it. If not, continue reading until you find a portion that is what you would like to say or feel. Worship God!

*Then **Repent***. Repenting has four components—*relenting, repenting, receiving*, and *resolving*:
- Pause to relent of any grudges or offenses that have separated you from others. We're told that if we withhold forgiveness, God won't forgive us (Mark 11:25).
- Prayerfully think about areas of sin that you're aware of and ask God to show you sin you might be overlooking. Repent—ask forgiveness with a heart to not repeat the sin—so that "though your sins are like scarlet, they shall be as white as snow; though they are red like crimson, they shall become like wool" (Isaiah 1:18).
- Gratefully accept God's forgiveness for your repented sin. We have His assurance that "if we confess our sins, he is faithful and just to forgive us our sins and to cleanse us from all unrighteousness" (1 John 1:9).

- With repentance comes resolving: accepting God's forgiveness and heeding Jesus' admonition to: "Go, and from now on sin no more" (John 8:11).

Now Ask! As a loving father, God gives good gifts to those who ask (Matthew 7:11). As you ask, endeavor to align your will to His—is what you're asking for His glory and your good? Ask.

Yield is the next step. Yielding is saying *"Yes!"* to God: "Yes" to what you want, "Yes" (or, "I am willing . . .") to what you don't want. In that way, you are saying "Yes" to His greater wisdom. As Jesus subjected His will to His Father, so must we. "Not my will, but yours, be done" (Luke 22:42b).

Pause to Express Thanks. We "give thanks to the LORD, for he is good" (Psalm 136:1a). You may want to start a gratitude journal to keep an ongoing list of God's goodness toward you.

Next, Rejoice. As you reach the end of your prayer time, the verses in this section provide assurance that God is your refuge. And there you can "Rejoice, always" (1 Thessalonians 5:16).

And, finally, Shalom. Shalom means peace. Close your prayer time in God's peace with a trusting "Amen." "Blessing and glory and wisdom and thanksgiving and honor and power and might be to our God forever and ever! Amen" (Revelation 7:12).

RESOURCES

Let people pray—earnestly, fervently, not simply morning and night, but the whole day long, making their lives one continued prayer.

ELIZABETH PRENTISS

Each day, pray for the people you've listed on that day's prayer list. You might find it helpful to leave this book or your own prayer notebook open in a convenient place to remind you to pray throughout your day. Record specific prayer requests or answers on the sheets provided, if you'd like.

If you'd prefer, consult one of the prayer theme guides. Each contains a month's list of daily topics to pray for a spouse, family, or for others.

SOME ALTERNATE ROUTES:

Seven Prayers

Psalm 119:164 says: "Seven times a day I praise you for your righteous rules." There is a sweet cadence in dividing our days into seven portions (as many religious orders have done for centuries). Instead of praying through the PathWay in one daily prayer time, consider dividing your day into seven prayer pauses. I've found it helpful to set the alarm on my phone to call me to prayer at seven points in my day. I either pray through one section of PRAYERS when the alarm rings, or I pray for a certain person or need.

Or you might benefit from focusing on one section of the PathWay for each day of the week.

Praying for Others

Prayer PathWay is helpful when praying in a focused way for a specific need or for a specific person; your prayer time can become a mini prayer retreat. Follow PRAYERS as you pray for that person or need. It works this way: Start

I always feel it well just to put a few words of prayer between everything I do.

CHARLES HADDON SPURGEON

by praising God for that person, then repent of any way you may have wronged that person, then make requests of God in relation to that person or need, and so on, continuing through each section of the path.

Train yourself to pray for a certain need or person while doing a specific daily task: when making the bed, pray for your spouse; when driving by your neighbors' house, pray for them; when brushing your teeth, pray for control of your mouth; when cooking, pray for spiritual sustenance for your relatives, and so on. As you weave your prayer time into your daily routines, and as you open your eyes and heart, you will be amazed to see how God inspires you to pray. It's humbling to realize that you might be the only one praying for a specific person or need. Soon, praying becomes an integral and effortless part of your daily tasks—the *main* thing!

Praying with Others

As you become familiar with Prayer PathWay, use it to pray *with* others, too. Family or small group worship times can become prayer excursions as you make a trip together through the path.

We are exhorted to: "Pray without ceasing" (1 Thessalonians 5:17), because God knows how much we need Him on this joyful, bewildering, sometimes dangerous, frequently arduous path of life.

Until you believe that life is war, you cannot know what prayer is for.

JOHN PIPER

You make known to me the path of life;
in your presence there is fullness of joy;
at your right hand are pleasures forevermore. (Psalm 16:11)

Each day represents a day trip—the accumulation of these fleeting days is our life's journey. Today is all I have! Either I will walk through this day in prayer, or I won't. I can't pray yesterday. I can't pray tomorrow. Today is all I have.

O Lord, make me know my end
and what is the measure of my days;
let me know how fleeting I am! (Psalm 39:4)

My hope and prayer for you, fellow sojourner, is that this guide will help you to tread a well-worn pathway of prayer, which God will use to guide you, to comfort you, to keep you from sin, to forgive you, to be your refuge, to give you peace; to give you Himself.

"The path of the righteous is like the light of dawn, which shines brighter and brighter until full day."
Proverbs 4:18

A GENTLE REMINDER
Please don't try to do all of *Prayer PathWay* at once. It's simply meant to be used as a guide in whatever way would be helpful now and to be adjusted for your future prayer needs.

THE PATH OF REDEMPTION

THE FACT THAT you're opening a book on prayer could mean that you already pray and are looking for some fresh encouragement; or that you want to pray and are seeking motivation; or that you want to want to pray (which, in itself, reveals a desire to pray!) and are searching for inspiration. Or it could mean that someone who loves you gave you this book because he or she wants you to pray, so you're giving it a try. In any case, welcome! I hope you'll join me on the path of prayer.

From an earthly perspective, a life of faith begins with prayer—and is sustained by prayer. Some Christians can remember the exact date of their first authentic prayer of faith—the day of their conversion. Others don't remember but have heard people (usually their parents) recount those first steps of faith. Others don't remember not being in faith; their memory is of always being in Christ. Any of those stories can reflect saving and authentic conversion, because our conversion is simply our seeing our need and God's meeting it.

Of course, none of us knows when his or her redemption really began because none of us was there! Our redemption began in the mind of God before creation. He made a plan. His Son was born to make it happen. Jesus walked our path of

This debt was so great that, while none but man must solve the debt, none but God was able to do it.

ANSELM

redemption right to the cross and has gone ahead of us into eternity. He is the Way and the destination. He is the path—and He is the prize!

Christ is the path and Christ the prize.

JOHN S. B. MONSELL

My plea to you is this: consider whether you've been redeemed by Christ, redeemed from your self-reliance and your self-made plans, saved from your sins, secured for eternity.

If you're a Christian, you'll often run to God for needful repentance (we'll talk about that later in this book). But if you aren't redeemed, that's the first thing to address. You may not know much about God, but you know about yourself. You know—deep down—that something is wrong. That sense is God drawing you. Listen.

You need what God has. He is what you need.

Your prayer of redemption needs no perfect words, just your acknowledgement of your sin, your awareness of God's solution, and your desire to surrender to Him.

Ponder these passages and pray your heart out to Him. Confess your sin and ask for forgiveness—and ask for the faith to believe all that God is and the strength to obey all that He asks.

All people are sinners. Sin separates us from God.

Your iniquities have made a separation between you and your God, and your sins have hidden his face from you so that he does not hear.
Isaiah 59:2

God's love made a plan.

God shows his love for us in that while we were still sinners, Christ died for us.
Romans 5:8

For the Son of Man came to seek and to save the lost.
Luke 19:10

In this is love, not that we have loved God but that he loved us and sent his Son to be the [perfect sacrifice] for our sins.
1 John 4:10

Redemption became necessary not because of what men were doing only, but because of what they were. . . . Fallen men acted in accord with what they were. Their hearts dictated their deeds.

A. W. TOZER

God promises to hear you when you call out to Him.

[Jesus says] Truly, truly, I say to you, whoever believes has eternal life.
John 6:47

If you confess with your mouth that Jesus is Lord and believe in your heart
that God raised him from the dead, you will be saved. For with the heart one
believes and is justified, and with the mouth one confesses and is saved.
Romans 10:9–10

Everyone who calls on the name of the Lord will be saved.
Romans 10:13

His response to you will be your redemption.

He has delivered us from the domain of darkness and transferred us to the kingdom of his beloved Son, in whom we have redemption, the forgiveness of sins.
Colossians 1:13–14

You will be new.

If anyone is in Christ, he is a new creation. The old has passed away; behold,
the new has come.
2 Corinthians 5:17

The result: you will have a new heart and the power of the Holy Spirit to cause you to walk in obedience. You will glorify God as you grow in Christ.

I will give you a new heart, and a new spirit I will put within you. And I will
remove the heart of stone from your flesh and give you a heart of flesh. And
I will put my Spirit within you, and cause you to walk in my statutes and be
careful to obey my rules.
Ezekiel 36:26–27

But grow in the grace and knowledge of our
Lord and Savior Jesus Christ. To him be the
glory both now and to the day of eternity.
Amen.
2 Peter 3:18

*Praying and sinning will
never live together in the same
heart. Prayer will consume
sin, or sin will choke prayer.*

J. C. RYLE

This is redemption:

But God, being rich in mercy, because of the great love with which he loved us, even when we were dead in our trespasses, made us alive together with Christ—by grace you have been saved—and raised us up with him and seated us with him in the heavenly places in Christ Jesus, so that in the coming ages he might show the immeasurable riches of his grace in kindness toward us in Christ Jesus. For by grace you have been saved through faith. And this is not your own doing; it is the gift of God, not a result of works, so that no one may boast. For we are his workmanship, created in Christ Jesus for good works, which God prepared beforehand, that we should walk in them.
Ephesians 2:4–10

Your salvation means that God's great love has redeemed you *from* your own wandering way and *for* His higher, holy way. You will have *His* peace and *His* purpose.

The Christian's journey is not on a smooth, flat highway—there are high mountains and deep valleys, bright mornings and dark nights of the soul. This is God's way to keep us praying—to keep us leaning on Him instead of darting off on our own. It's His way! It's the way of glory.

The path of the righteous is like the light of dawn, which shines brighter and brighter until full day.
Proverbs 4:18

So now, fellow traveler,
join me on a pathway of prayer.

Prayer of Invocation

Dear Father, Son, and Holy Spirit:

We know that *You hear us, Father; You stand interceding for us, Christ; You groan for us, Holy Spirit.* You know us better than we know ourselves. Sometimes we are eager and expectant in prayer—and sometimes we are reluctant and skeptical. But we know this: we have nowhere else to go! You *have* what we need; You *are* what we need. You *know* our path; You *are* our way. So we say with the disciples, humbly and desperately, "Lord, teach us to pray!"

I am longing to pray.

Amen.

"You make known to me the path of life; in your presence there is
fullness of joy; at your right hand are pleasures forevermore."
Psalm 16:11

PART 2

PRAYERS

REPENT   ASK   YIELD   EXPRESS THANKS   REJOICE   SHALOM.

The LORD reigns

. . . .

Yes, the world is established;
it shall never be moved.
Your throne is established from of old;
you are from everlasting.

PSALM 93:1–2

Keep me at all times
from robbing thee,
and from depriving my soul
of thy due worship.

THE VALLEY OF VISION

PRAISE

God Is Enthroned

WE WERE CREATED TO WORSHIP. We will either worship God or we'll worship His creation, which is idolatry. All of God's creation was made to praise Him. Psalm 148 describes this beautifully:

Praise the LORD!
Praise the LORD from the heavens;
    praise him in the heights!
Praise him, all his angels;
    praise him, all his hosts!

Praise him, sun and moon,
    praise him, all you shining stars!
Praise him, you highest heavens,
    and you waters above the heavens! (vv. 1–4)

Praise the LORD from the earth,
    you great sea creatures and all deeps,
fire and hail, snow and mist,
    stormy wind fulfilling his word!

Mountains and all hills,
    fruit trees and all cedars!

A soul redeemed demands a life of praise.
WILLIAM COWPER

Beasts and all livestock,
    creeping things and flying birds!

Kings of the earth and all peoples,
    princes and all rulers of the earth!
Young men and maidens together,
    old men and children! (vv. 7–12)

Praise the LORD! (v. 14b)

> *Let everything that has*
> *breath praise the LORD!*
> PSALM 150:6a

All that God created is mentioned: angels, the heavens, sun and moon and stars, animals, the elements, earth and plants and trees, people both young and old. In praising God, we are joining His people who have, over the centuries, lifted their hearts and voices in worship. Children, young people, old people, mystics, pragmatics—in days of ease or years of suffering, free or imprisoned, healthy or ill, rich or poor. God's people have praised Him everywhere: in homes and in catacombs, in prisons and in hospitals, in caves and in meadows, in airplanes and in taxis, in synagogues and in church buildings.

The condition of our life, the location of our body, or the mood of our spirit doesn't determine our praise—our being does. We were created to praise.

To praise God is to proclaim my admiration of Him. It is to take my focus off of myself to think about Him: His attributes, His works, His steadfastness. *Praise is pushing back my daily worries and impending tasks to acknowledge my always present, never-changing God.* Setting my mind's attention and my heart's affection Godward leads to praise.

> *In commanding*
> *us to glorify Him,*
> *God is inviting us*
> *to enjoy Him.*
> C.S. LEWIS

ASSUMING A POSTURE OF PRAISE

We are a casual culture. We have little experience with the formality that is due a king. As His children, there are times when we can race into the throne room and implore our Father about a pressing need but, for the most part, our posture in worship should be one of reverence. In the Bible, God is always approached in prayer with humility. The posture of our physical body helps focus our worship, but it is the posture of the heart that is crucial. In worship, we are approaching the Almighty God!

- God said to Moses: "Take your sandals off your feet, for the place on which you are standing is holy ground" (Exodus 3:5).
- The angels in Isaiah covered their faces in praise: "Each [seraphim] had six wings: with two he covered his face, and with two he covered his feet, and with two he flew" (Isaiah 6:2).
- Paul reminds us "that at the name of Jesus every knee should bow, in heaven and on earth and under the earth" (Philippians 2:10).

At times, our praise comes effortlessly; at times praise is a decision, an act of the will, an obedient response to God's surpassing worthiness. God does not require us to praise Him in a formulaic fashion. We can praise Him just as honestly in despair as in joy.

- We can praise God in simple, overflowing awe, as Mary did: "My soul magnifies the Lord, and my spirit rejoices in God my Savior" (Luke 1:46–47).
- We can praise God in suffering, as Paul and Silas did in jail: "About midnight Paul and Silas were praying and singing hymns to God" (Acts 16:25a).
- We can praise as we ponder a passage such as: "Ah, Lord GOD! It is you who have made the heavens and the earth by your great power and by your outstretched arm! Nothing is too hard for you" (Jeremiah 32:17).
- We can praise by whispering a phrase: "Blessed be the name of God forever and ever" (Daniel 2:20b).
- We can praise by uttering a name of God: El Shaddai (Almighty One), El Elyon (The Most High God), Adonai (Master). See page 34.

    God said: "I am the LORD your God."
    LEVITICUS 18:4B

- We can praise by meditating on an attribute of God: "The LORD is merciful" (Psalm 103:8a). See pages 36–37.
- We can praise by musing over the "I am" statements of Christ: "I am the Bread of Life," "I am the Light of the world," and so on. See page 34.

    This is my beloved Son, with whom I am well pleased.
    MATTHEW 3:17

Table 1. Some Names of God

Elohim	He is Creator	Genesis 1:1
El-Elyon	He is God Most High	Genesis 14:19b
El-Olam	He is the Everlasting God	Isaiah 40:28
El-Roi	He is the One Who Sees	Genesis 16:13
El-Shaddai	He is God Almighty	Genesis 17:1
Adonai	He is Lord Almighty	Deuteronomy 10:17
Jehovah-Jireh	He is the Provider	Genesis 22:14
Jehovah-Maccaddeshem	He is the Sanctifier	Exodus 31:13
Jehovah-Nissi	He is our Banner	Exodus 17:15
Jehovah-Rapha	He is the Healer	Exodus 15:26
Jehovah-Sabbaoth	He is the Lord of Hosts	Psalm 23:1
Jehovah-Rohi	He is the Shepherd	Isaiah 6:1–3
Jehovah-Shalom	He is Peace	Judges 6:24
Jehovah-Shammah	He is the Lord Who is Present	Ezekiel 48:35
Jehovah-Azar	He is my Helper	Psalm 54:4

Table 2. The "I AM" Statements of Christ

Jesus said: "I am **the bread of life**."	John 6:48
Jesus said: "I am **the light of the world**."	John 9:5b
Jesus said: "I am **the door**."	John 10:7b
Jesus said: "I am **the good shepherd**."	John 10:11a
Jesus said: "I am **the resurrection and the life**."	John 11:25a
Jesus said: "I am **the way, the truth and the life**."	John 14:6a
Jesus said: "I am **the vine**."	John 15:5a

- We can praise in song, as the Israelites did: "Then Moses and the people of Israel sang this song to the LORD, saying, 'I will sing to the LORD, for he has triumphed gloriously; the horse and his rider he has thrown into the sea. The LORD is my strength and my song, and he has become my salvation; this is my God, and I will praise him, my father's God, and I will exalt him'" (Exodus 15:1–2).
- We can praise God by crying out His greatness: "For great is the LORD, and greatly to be praised" (Psalm 96:4a).
- We can praise God by reminding ourselves to praise Him: "I call upon the LORD, who is worthy to be praised" (2 Samuel 22:4a).

Great are You, O Lord, and greatly to be praised; great is Your power, and Your wisdom is infinite. And You would man praise; man, that is but a particle of Your creation; man, that bears about him his mortality.

AUGUSTINE OF HIPPO

Starting my prayer time with praise helps me to adjust my focus; to catch a glimpse of the eternal instead of being mired in the temporal. It reminds me that God is God, and I am not.

PATH MARKER
Read through the *Praise* verses until you feel your heart say: "Yes— that's what I'm trying to say!" and echo those words of praise. If you're able, don't rush away—let your heart wander to worship.

GOD IS . . .

GOD IS **HOLY**

It is written, "You shall be holy, for I am holy."
1 Peter 1:16

God said: "I
AM WHO I AM."

EXODUS 3:14

GOD IS **UNCHANGING**

For I the LORD do not change.
Malachi 3:6a

GOD IS **COMPASSIONATE**

As a father shows compassion to his children, so the LORD shows compassion to those who fear him.
Psalm 103:13

GOD IS **STEADFAST**

Give thanks to the God of heaven, for his steadfast love endures forever.
Psalm 136:26

GOD IS **PATIENT**

The Lord is not slow to fulfill his promise as some count slowness, but is patient toward you, not wishing that any should perish, but that all should reach repentance.
2 Peter 3:9

GOD IS **LOVING**

God is love.
1 John 4:8b

GOD IS **FORGIVING**

As far as the east is from the west, so far does he remove our transgressions from us.

Psalm 103:12

GOD IS **FAITHFUL**

Know therefore that the LORD your God is God, the faithful God who keeps covenant and steadfast love with those who love him and keep his commandments, to a thousand generations.

Deuteronomy 7:9

GOD IS **SOVEREIGN**

I am God, and there is none like me, declaring the end from the beginning and from ancient times things not yet done, saying, "My counsel shall stand, and I will accomplish all my purpose."

Isaiah 46:9b–10

GOD IS **OMNISCIENT**

You know when I sit down and when I rise up; you discern my thoughts from afar.

Psalm 139:2

GOD IS **OMNIPRESENT**

Where shall I go from your Spirit? Or where shall I flee from your presence? If I ascend to heaven, you are there! If I make my bed in Sheol, you are there!

Psalm 139:7

GOD IS **OMNIPOTENT**

Is anything too hard for the LORD?

Genesis 18:14

A PRAYER OF PRAISE

Dear Mighty Father, Reigning Son, and
Abiding Holy Spirit:

You are over the whole universe—over every particle, every atom.
You speak and summon the earth from the rising of its sun to its setting.
You shine forth. You are the Creator of life and the Sustainer of faith.
You are eternally praised with or without us—all creation, from life-
less stone to shining angel, praises You. I want to be part of the echoing
anthem that reverberates across the ages and into eternity. May my life
be a doxology. You, the Mighty One, are enthroned on my small praises.
Great are You, God!

I am in awe.

Amen.

> *"The Mighty One, God the LORD, speaks and summons*
> *the earth from the rising of the sun to its setting. Out of*
> *Zion, the perfection of beauty, God shines forth."*
> *Psalm 50:1–2*

PRAYER PASSAGES

The LORD is my strength and my song, and he has become my salvation; this is my God, and I will praise him, my father's God, and I will exalt him. . . . Who is like you, O LORD, among the gods? Who is like you, majestic in holiness, awesome in glorious deeds, doing wonders?

Exodus 15:2, 11

He is your praise. He is your God.

Deuteronomy 10:21a

There is none holy like the LORD: for there is none besides you; there is no rock like our God.

1 Samuel 2:2

The LORD is my rock and my fortress and my deliverer, my God, my rock, in whom I take refuge, my shield, and the horn of my salvation, my stronghold and my refuge, my savior. . . . I call upon the LORD, who is worthy to be praised.

2 Samuel 22:2–4a

This God—his way is perfect; the word of the LORD proves true; he is a shield for all those who take refuge in him. For who is God, but the LORD? And who is a rock, except our God? This God is my strong refuge and has made my way blameless. He made my feet like the feet of a deer and set me secure on the heights. . . . You have given me the shield of your salvation, and your gentleness made me great.

2 Samuel 22:31–34, 36

If we are to pray aright, perhaps it is quite necessary that we pray contrary to our own heart. Not what we want to pray is important, but what God wants us to pray. If we were dependent entirely on ourselves, we would probably pray only the fourth petition of the Lord's Prayer. But God wants it otherwise. The richness of the Word of God ought to determine our prayer, not the poverty of our heart.

DIETRICH BONHOEFFER

39

The LORD lives, and blessed be my rock, and exalted be my God, the rock of my salvation. . . . For this I will praise you, O LORD, among the nations, and sing praises to your name.

2 Samuel 22:47, 50

O LORD, God of Israel, there is no God like you, in heaven above or on earth beneath, keeping covenant and showing steadfast love to your servants who walk before you with all their heart.

1 Kings 8:23

O LORD, the God of Israel, enthroned above the cherubim, you are the God, you alone, of all the kingdoms of the earth; you have made heaven and earth.

2 Kings 19:15b

Oh give thanks to the LORD; call upon his name; make known his deeds among the peoples! Sing to him, sing praises to him; tell of all his wondrous works! Glory in his holy name; let the hearts of those who seek the LORD rejoice! Seek the LORD and his strength; seek his presence continually!

1 Chronicles 16:8–11

For great is the LORD, and greatly to be praised, and he is to be feared above all gods. For all the gods of the peoples are worthless idols, but the LORD made the heavens. Splendor and majesty are before him; strength and joy are in his place. Ascribe to the LORD, O families of the peoples, ascribe to the LORD glory and strength! Ascribe to the LORD the glory due his name; bring an offering and come before him! Worship the LORD in the splendor of holiness; tremble before him, all the earth; yes, the world is established; it shall

*Holy, holy, holy! Lord
    God Almighty!
Early in the morning our
    song shall rise to Thee;
Holy, holy, holy, merciful
    and mighty!
God in three Persons,
    blessed Trinity!*

REGINALD HEBER

*It is He who brought us
out of guilt and into
    forgiveness,
out of darkness into light,
out of . . . rebellion and
    into Your love,
out of death and into life.*

JOHN MACARTHUR

never be moved. Let the heavens be glad, and
let the earth rejoice, and let them say among the
nations, "The LORD reigns!"
1 Chronicles 16:25–31

Blessed are you, O LORD, the God of Israel our
father, forever and ever. Yours, O LORD, is the
greatness and the power and the glory and the victory and the majesty, for all that is in the heavens
and in the earth is yours. Yours is the kingdom, O
LORD, and you are exalted as head above all.
1 Chronicles 29:10b–11

And I said, "O LORD God of heaven, the great
and awesome God who keeps covenant and steadfast love with those who love him and keep his
commandments, let your ear be attentive and your
eyes open, to hear the prayer of your servant."
Nehemiah 1:5–6a

Stand up and bless the LORD your God from
everlasting to everlasting. Blessed be your glorious
name, which is exalted above all blessing and praise.
Nehemiah 9:5b

You are the LORD, you alone. You have made
heaven, the heaven of heavens, with all their
host, the earth and all that is on it, the seas and all
that is in them; and you preserve all of them; and
the host of heaven worships you.
Nehemiah 9:6

As for me, I would seek God, and to God would I
commit my cause, who does great things and
unsearchable, marvelous things without number.
Job 5:8–9

God is most glorified
in us when we are most
satisfied in Him.
JOHN PIPER

You awaken us to delight
in Your praise; for You
made us for Yourself, and
our heart is restless, until
it reposes in You.
AUGUSTINE OF
HIPPO

I bind unto myself today
The strong Name of the
  Trinity,
By invocation of the same,
The Three in One,
and One in Three.
I bind this day to me
  forever,
By power of faith,
Christ's incarnation;
His baptism in the Jordan
  River;
His death on the cross
for my salvation.
His bursting from
  the spiced tomb;
His riding up
  the Heav'nly way;
His coming at
  the day of doom:
I bind unto myself today.

PATRICK OF
IRELAND

O Lord, our Lord, how majestic is your name
in all the earth! You have set your glory above
the heavens. . . . When I look at your heavens,
the work of your fingers, the moon and the stars,
which you have set in place, what is man that
you are mindful of him, and the son of man that
you care for him? Yet you have made him a little
lower than the heavenly beings and crowned him
with glory and honor. . . . O Lord, our Lord, how
majestic is your name in all the earth!
Psalm 8:1, 3–5, 9

I will give thanks to the Lord with my whole
heart; I will recount all of your wonderful deeds.
I will be glad and exult in you; I will sing praise to
your name, O Most High.
Psalm 9:1–2

The Lord sits enthroned forever.
Psalm 9:7a

The law of the Lord is perfect, reviving the soul;
the testimony of the Lord is sure, making wise
the simple; the precepts of the Lord are right,
rejoicing the heart; the commandment of the
Lord is pure, enlightening the eyes; the fear of
the Lord is clean, enduring forever; the rules of
the Lord are true, and righteous altogether. More
to be desired are they than gold, even much fine
gold; sweeter also than honey and drippings of the
honeycomb. Moreover, by them is your servant
warned; in keeping them there is great reward.
Psalm 19:7–11

Be exalted, O Lord, in your strength! We will sing and praise your power.
Psalm 21:13

Yet you are holy, enthroned on the praises of Israel.
Psalm 22:3

The earth is the Lord's and the fullness thereof, the world and those who dwell therein.
Psalm 24:1

You have said, "Seek my face." My heart says to you, "Your face, Lord, do I seek."
Psalm 27:8

Ascribe to the Lord, O heavenly beings, ascribe to the Lord glory and strength. Ascribe to the Lord the glory due his name; worship the Lord in the splendor of holiness.
Psalm 29:1–2

I will bless the Lord at all times; his praise shall continually be in my mouth. My soul makes its boast in the Lord; let the humble hear and be glad. Oh, magnify the Lord with me, and let us exalt his name together! I sought the Lord, and he answered me and delivered me from all my fears.
Psalms 34:1–4

By day the Lord commands his steadfast love, and at night his song is with me, a prayer to the God of my life.
Psalm 42:8

Praise is the rehearsal of our eternal song.

CHARLES HADDON SPURGEON

*To Thee our morning song
    of praise,
To Thee our evening
    prayer we raise;
O grant us with Thy
    saints on high
To praise Thee through
    eternity.*

AMBROSE OF MILAN

Be still, and know that I am God. I will be exalted among the nations, I will be exalted in the earth!
Psalm 46:10

O my Strength, I will watch for you, for you,
O God, are my fortress. My God in his steadfast
love will meet me.
Psalm 59:9–10a

For God alone my soul waits in silence; from him
comes my salvation. He only is my rock and my
salvation, my fortress; I shall not be greatly shaken.
Psalm 62:1–2

O God, you are my God; earnestly I seek you; my
soul thirsts for you; my flesh faints for you, as in a
dry and weary land where there is no water. So I have
looked upon you in the sanctuary, beholding your
power and glory. Because your steadfast love is better
than life, my lips will praise you. So I will bless you
as long as I live; in your name I will lift up my hands.
Psalm 63:1–4

Shout for joy to God, all the earth; sing the glory
of his name; give to him glorious praise! Say to
God, "How awesome are your deeds!"
Psalm 66:1–3a

O kingdoms of the earth, sing to God; sing
praises to the Lord, *Selah* to him who rides in the
heavens, the ancient heavens; behold, he sends out
his voice, his mighty voice. Ascribe power to God,
whose majesty is over Israel, and whose power is in
the skies. Awesome is God from his sanctuary; the
God of Israel—he is the one who gives power and
strength to his people. Blessed be God!
Psalm 68:32–35

*Praise lies upon a higher
plane than thanksgiving.
When I give thanks,
my thoughts still circle
around myself to some
extent. But in praise
my soul ascends to
self-forgetting adoration,
seeing and praising only
the majesty and power
of God, His grace and
redemption.*

OLE HALLESBY

Yours is the day, yours also the night; you have
established the heavenly lights and the sun.
Psalm 74:16

Your way, O God, is holy. What god is great like
our God? You are the God who works wonders; you
have made known your might among the peoples.
Psalm 77:13–14

All the nations you have made shall come and
worship before you, O Lord, and shall glorify your
name. For you are great and do wondrous
things; you alone are God.
Psalm 86:9–10

The LORD reigns; he is robed in majesty; the
LORD is robed; he has put on strength as his belt.
Yes, the world is established; it shall never be
moved. Your throne is established from of old; you
are from everlasting.
Psalm 93:1–2

Oh come, let us sing to the LORD; let us make a
joyful noise to the rock of our salvation! Let us
come into his presence with thanksgiving; let us
make a joyful noise to him with songs of praise!
For the LORD is a great God, and a great King
above all gods. In his hand are the depths of the
earth; the heights of the mountains are his also.
The sea is his, for he made it, and his hands formed
the dry land. Oh come, let us worship and bow
down; let us kneel before the LORD, our Maker!
Psalm 95:1–6

The LORD reigns, let the earth rejoice.
Psalm 97:1a

*It is the adoring worship
of God, the waiting on
Him and for Him, the
deep silence of the soul
that yields itself for God
to reveal Himself, that
the capacity for knowing
and trusting God will
be developed. It is as we
take His Word from the
Blessed Book, and bring
it to Himself, asking Him
to speak it to us with His
living loving voice, that
the power will come fully
to believe and receive the
word as God's own to us.*
ANDREW MURRAY

Oh sing to the LORD a new song, for he has done marvelous things! His right hand and his holy arm have worked salvation for him. The LORD has made known his salvation; he has revealed his righteousness in the sight of the nations. He has remembered his steadfast love and faithfulness to the house of Israel. All the ends of the earth have seen the salvation of our God. Make a joyful noise to the LORD, all the earth; break forth into joyous song and sing praises!
Psalm 98:1–4

The LORD reigns; let the peoples tremble! He sits enthroned upon the cherubim; let the earth quake! The LORD is great in Zion; he is exalted over all the peoples. Let them praise your great and awesome name! Holy is he! The King in his might loves justice. You have established equity; you have executed justice and righteousness in Jacob. Exalt the LORD our God; worship at his footstool! Holy is he!
Psalm 99:1–5

Make a joyful noise to the LORD, all the earth! Serve the LORD with gladness! Come into his presence with singing! Know that the LORD, he is God! It is he who made us, and we are his; we are his people, and the sheep of his pasture. Enter his gates with thanksgiving, and his courts with praise! Give thanks to him; bless his name! For the LORD is good; his steadfast love endures forever, and his faithfulness to all generations.
Psalm 100

But you, O LORD, are enthroned forever; you are remembered throughout all generations.
Psalm 102:12

*Thou, fairest, greatest,
first of all objects,
my heart admires, adores,
loves thee,
for my little vessel is as
full as it can be,
and I would pour out all
that fullness before thee
in ceaseless flow. . . .
Increase my love, O my
God, through time and
eternity.*

THE VALLEY OF
VISION

46

Bless the LORD, O my soul, and all that is within me, bless his holy name!
Psalm 103:1

Bless the LORD, O my soul! O LORD my God, you are very great! You are clothed with splendor and majesty, covering yourself with light as with a garment, stretching out the heavens like a tent.
Psalm 104:1–2

May the glory of the LORD endure forever; may the LORD rejoice in his works, who looks on the earth and it trembles, who touches the mountains and they smoke! I will sing to the LORD as long as I live; I will sing praise to my God while I have being. May my meditation be pleasing to him, for I rejoice in the LORD.
Psalm 104:31–34

I will give thanks to you, O LORD, among the peoples; I will sing praises to you among the nations. For your steadfast love is great above the heavens; your faithfulness reaches to the clouds. Be exalted, O God, above the heavens! Let your glory be over all the earth!
Psalm 108:3–5

Praise the LORD! I will give thanks to the LORD with my whole heart, in the company of the upright, in the congregation. Great are the works of the LORD, studied by all who delight in them. Full of splendor and majesty is his work, and his righteousness endures forever. He has caused his wondrous works to be remembered; the LORD is gracious and merciful. He provides food for those who fear him; he remembers his covenant forever.
Psalm 111:1–5

Called by the Spirit, I enter thy presence, worshipping thee with godly fear, awed by thy majesty, greatness, glory, but encouraged by thy love.
THE VALLEY OF VISION

The more you praise, the more vigor you will have for prayer; and the more you pray, the more matter you will have for praise.
J. I. PACKER

Praise the LORD! Praise, O servants of the LORD,
praise the name of the LORD! Blessed be the name
of the LORD from this time forth and forevermore! From the rising of the sun to its setting, the
name of the LORD is to be praised!
Psalm 113:1–3

Not to us, O LORD, not to us, but to your name
give glory, for the sake of your steadfast love and
your faithfulness! Why should the nations say,
"Where is their God?" Our God is in the heavens;
he does all that he pleases.
Psalm 115:1–3

But we will bless the LORD from this time forth
and forevermore. Praise the LORD!
Psalm 115:18

I love the LORD, because he has heard my voice
and my pleas for mercy. Because he inclined his ear
to me, therefore I will call on him as long as I live.
Psalm 116:1–2

Gracious is the LORD, and righteous; our God is
merciful.
Psalm 116:5

Praise the LORD, all nations! Extol him, all
peoples! For great is his steadfast love toward us,
and the faithfulness of the LORD endures forever.
Praise the LORD!
Psalm 117:1–2

Forever, O LORD, your word is firmly fixed in the
heavens. Your faithfulness endures to all generations;
you have established the earth, and it stands fast.
Psalm 119:89–90

*O LORD, I believe, I
adore, and I love; I
beseech Thee to increase
my faith, and to fill
my heart with loving
adoration and adoring
love; for Thy mercies' sake,
O Lord. — Amen.*
MARY WILDER
TILESTON

*Impress me deeply with a
sense of thine
omnipresence, that thou
art about my path,
my ways, my lying down,
my end.*
THE VALLEY OF
VISION

48

Seven times a day I praise you for your righteous rules. Great peace have those who love your law; nothing can make them stumble.

Psalm 119:164–65

I will extol you, my God and King, and bless your name forever and ever. Every day I will bless you and praise your name forever and ever. Great is the LORD, and greatly to be praised, and his greatness is unsearchable. . . . The LORD is gracious and merciful, slow to anger and abounding in steadfast love. The LORD is good to all, and his mercy is over all that he has made. All your works shall give thanks to you, O LORD, and all your saints shall bless you!

Psalm 145:1–3, 8–10

Praise the LORD! For it is good to sing praises to our God; for it is pleasant, and a song of praise is fitting. . . . He heals the brokenhearted and binds up their wounds. He determines the number of the stars; he gives to all of them their names. Great is our Lord, and abundant in power; his understanding is beyond measure.

Psalm 147:1, 3–5

Praise the LORD! Praise the LORD from the heavens; praise him in the heights! Praise him, all his angels; praise him, all his hosts! Praise him, sun and moon, praise him, all you shining stars! Praise him, you highest heavens, and you waters above the heavens! Let them praise the name of the LORD! For he commanded and they were created. And he established them forever and ever; he gave a decree, and it shall not pass away.

Psalm 148:1–6

The trivial round, the
common task,
Will furnish all we ought
to ask;
Room to deny ourselves, a
road
To bring us daily nearer
God.
Only, O Lord, in Thy
dear love,
Fit us for perfect rest
above,
And help us, this and
every day,
To live more nearly as we
pray.

JOHN KEBLE

Young men and maidens together, old men and children! Let them praise the name of the LORD, for his name alone is exalted; his majesty is above earth and heaven.

Psalm 148:12–13

Praise the LORD! Praise God in his sanctuary; praise him in his mighty heavens! Praise him for his mighty deeds; praise him according to his excellent greatness! . . . Let everything that has breath praise the LORD! Praise the LORD!

Psalm 150:1–2, 6

Holy, holy, holy is the LORD of hosts; the whole earth is full of his glory!

Isaiah 6:3b

O LORD, you are my God; I will exalt you; I will praise your name, for you have done wonderful things, plans formed of old, faithful and sure.

Isaiah 25:1

Lift up your eyes on high and see: who created these? He who brings out their host by number, calling them all by name, by the greatness of his might, and because he is strong in power not one is missing.

Isaiah 40:26

Have you not known? Have you not heard? The LORD is the everlasting God, the Creator of the ends of the earth. He does not faint or grow weary; his understanding is unsearchable. He gives power to the faint, and to him who has no might he increases strength.

Isaiah 40:28–29

Glory be to Thee, O GOD, the Father, the Maker of the World.
Glory be to Thee, O GOD, the Son, the Redeemer of mankind.
Glory be to Thee, O GOD, the Holy Ghost, the Sanctifier of Thy people.

BROOKE FOSS
WESTCOTT

Sing, O heavens, for the LORD has done it; shout,
O depths of the earth; break forth into singing, O
mountains, O forest, and every tree in it! For the
LORD has redeemed Jacob, and will be glorified
in Israel. Thus says the LORD, your Redeemer,
who formed you from the womb: "I am the LORD,
who made all things, who alone stretched out the
heavens, who spread out the earth by myself."
Isaiah 44:23–24

I am the LORD your God, who stirs up the sea so
that its waves roar—the LORD of hosts is his name.
Isaiah 51:15

For thus says the One who is high and lifted up,
who inhabits eternity, whose name is Holy: "I dwell
in the high and holy place, and also with him who
is of a contrite and lowly spirit, to revive the spirit
of the lowly, and to revive the heart of the contrite."
Isaiah 57:15

Thus says the LORD: "Heaven is my throne, and
the earth is my footstool; what is the house that
you would build for me, and what is the place of my
rest? All these things my hand has made, and so all
these things came to be, declares the LORD. But
this is the one to whom I will look: he who is humble and contrite in spirit and trembles at my word."
Isaiah 66:1–2

There is none like you, O LORD; you are great,
and your name is great in might. Who would not
fear you, O King of the nations? For this is your
due; for among all the wise ones of the nations
and in all their kingdoms there is none like you.
Jeremiah 10:6–7

*My life and death belong
to thee,
For I am thine, O God;
Thy hands have made
and fashioned me,
'Tis thine to bear the load.*

GEORGE
MACDONALD

*Christ made the beauty of
the world, and he made
men that they might
enjoy that beauty and
celebrate it unto his praise.*

J. GRESHAM MACHEN

I will give them a heart to know that I am the Lord, and they shall be my people and I will be their God, for they shall return to me with their whole heart.

Jeremiah 24:7

Ah, Lord God! It is you who have made the heavens and the earth by your great power and by your outstretched arm! Nothing is too hard for you.

Jeremiah 32:17

Blessed be the name of God forever and ever, to whom belong wisdom and might. He changes times and seasons; he removes kings and sets up kings; he gives wisdom to the wise and knowledge to those who have understanding; he reveals deep and hidden things; he knows what is in the darkness, and the light dwells with him. To you, O God of my fathers, I give thanks and praise.

Daniel 2:20b–23a

For behold, he who forms the mountains and creates the wind, and declares to man what is his thought, who makes the morning darkness, and treads on the heights of the earth—the Lord, the God of hosts, is his name!

Amos 4:13

For the earth will be filled with the knowledge of the glory of the Lord as the waters cover the sea.

Habakkuk 2:14

The Lord is in his holy temple; let all the earth keep silence before him.

Habakkuk 2:20

The Lord your God is in your midst, a mighty one who will save; he will rejoice over you with

We know that God is everywhere; but certainly we feel his presence most when his worlds are on the grandest scale spread before us; and it is in the unclouded night-sky, where his worlds wheel their silent course, that we sense clearest his infinitude, his omnipotence, his omnipresence.

CHARLOTTE
BRONTË

gladness; he will quiet you by his love; he will exult over you with loud singing.
Zephaniah 3:17

Pray then like this: "Our Father in heaven, hallowed be your name. Your kingdom come, your will be done, on earth as it is in heaven."
Matthew 6:9–10

And Mary said, "My soul magnifies the Lord, and my spirit rejoices in God my Savior, for he has looked on the humble estate of his servant."
Luke 1:46–48a

Jesus answered him, "It is written, 'You shall worship the Lord your God, and him only shall you serve.'"
Luke 4:8

God is spirit, and those who worship him must worship in spirit and truth.
John 4:24

The God who made the world and everything in it, being Lord of heaven and earth, does not live in temples made by man, nor is he served by human hands, as though he needed anything, since he himself gives to all mankind life and breath and everything . . . for in him we live and move and have our being.
Acts 17:24–25, 28a

Oh, the depth of the riches and wisdom and knowledge of God! How unsearchable are his judgments and how inscrutable his ways! "For who has known the mind of the Lord, or who has been his counselor? Or who has given a gift to him that he might be repaid?" For from him and through him and to him are all things. To him be glory forever. Amen.
Romans 11:33–36

Praise God, from whom
  all blessings flow;
Praise Him, all creatures
  here below;
Praise Him above, O
  heavenly host;
Praise Father, Son, and
  Holy Ghost. Amen.
THOMAS KEN

O worship the King,
  all glorious above,
O gratefully sing
  God's power and God's
  love;
Our Shield and Defender,
  the Ancient of Days,
Pavilioned in splendor,
  and girded with praise.
ROBERT GRANT

Yet for us there is one God, the Father, from whom are all things and for whom we exist, and one Lord, Jesus Christ, through whom are all things and through whom we exist.

1 Corinthians 8:6

What am I to do? I will pray with my spirit, but I will pray with my mind also; I will sing praise with my spirit, but I will sing with my mind also.

1 Corinthians 14:15

Blessed be the God and Father of our Lord Jesus Christ, who has blessed us in Christ with every spiritual blessing in the heavenly places.

Ephesians 1:3

Therefore God has highly exalted him and bestowed on him the name that is above every name, so that at the name of Jesus every knee should bow, in heaven and on earth and under the earth, and every tongue confess that Jesus Christ is Lord, to the glory of God the Father.

Philippians 2:9–11

[Jesus] is the image of the invisible God, the firstborn of all creation. For by him all things were created, in heaven and on earth, visible and invisible, whether thrones or dominions or rulers or authorities—all things were created through him and for him. And he is before all things, and in him all things hold together. And he is the head of the body, the church. He is the beginning, the firstborn from the dead, that in everything he might be preeminent. For in him all the fullness of God was pleased to dwell, and through him to reconcile to himself all things,

While Jesus is representing me in heaven, may I reflect him on earth, While he pleads my cause, may I show forth his praise.

THE VALLEY OF VISION

We may ignore, but we can nowhere evade, the presence of God. The world is crowded with him. He walks everywhere incognito.

C.S. LEWIS

whether on earth or in heaven, making peace by the blood of his cross.

Colossians 1:15–20

Jesus Christ is the same yesterday and today and forever. . . . Through him then let us continually offer up a sacrifice of praise to God, that is, the fruit of lips that acknowledge his name.

Hebrews 13:8, 13

"I am the Alpha and the Omega," says the Lord God, "who is and who was and who is to come, the Almighty."

Revelation 1:8

Holy, holy, holy, is the Lord God Almighty, who was and is and is to come! . . . Worthy are you, our Lord and God, to receive glory and honor and power, for you created all things, and by your will they existed and were created.

Revelation 4:8b, 11

Worthy is the Lamb who was slain, to receive power and wealth and wisdom and might and honor and glory and blessing! . . . To him who sits on the throne and to the Lamb be blessing and honor and glory and might forever and ever!

Revelation 5:12, 13b

Great and amazing are your deeds, O Lord God the Almighty! Just and true are your ways, O King of the nations! Who will not fear, O Lord, and glorify your name? For you alone are holy. All nations will come and worship you, for your righteous acts have been revealed.

Revelation 15:3b–4

May I adore the mystery I cannot comprehend.
SUSANNA WESLEY

When God has all that He should have of thy heart, when thou art wholly given up to the obedience of the light and spirit of God within thee, to will only in His will, to love only in His love, to be wise only in His wisdom, then it is that everything thou does is as a song of praise, and the common business of the life is a conforming to God's will on earth as angels do in heaven.
WILLIAM LAW

Then I heard what seemed to be the voice of a
great multitude, like the roar of many waters
and like the sound of mighty peals of thunder,
crying out, "Hallelujah! For the Lord our God the
Almighty reigns."
Revelation 19:6

And I heard a loud voice from the throne saying,
"Behold, the dwelling place of God is with man.
He will dwell with them, and they will be his
people, and God himself will be with them as
their God."
Revelation 21:3

*Yea, let my whole life be
One anthem unto Thee,
And let the praise of lip
    and life
Outring all sin and strife.*
FRANCES HAVERGAL

*If we were trying to fill up
a silver cup of reverence to
the most holy name of our
Father God whom we can
call Father because of the
active obedience of Jesus
Christ as well as because
of His death, that cup
would* never *spill over.*
EDITH SCHAEFFER

Additional Verses

Additional Verses

If you, O LORD, should
mark iniquities,
O Lord, who could stand?
But with you there is forgiveness,
that you may be feared.

PSALM 130:3-4

Christ Jesus came into the
world to save sinners.

1 TIMOTHY 1:15b

I remember two things:
that I am a great sinner and
that Christ is a great savior.

JOHN NEWTON

REPENT

God Forgives

WE ARE SINNERS. If we are Christ's, we are redeemed, and yet, as Robert M'Cheyne said: "There is peace with God, but constant war with sin."

As sinners, we can take comfort in the fact that, in His earthly life, Jesus continually sought out people like us. He traveled with them, ate with them, taught them—He lived His life with them. Jesus was often criticized for His choice of companions. The Gospels record His preference to be with the sinners rather than the Pharisees (who were also sinners but thought they were not).

Come, ye sinners, poor and needy,
Weak and wounded, sick and sore;
Jesus ready stands to save you,
Full of pity, love and power.
JOSEPH HART

Mark described one of these events—it would have been shocking in Hebraic culture of that day:

> As [Jesus] reclined at table . . . many tax collectors and sinners were reclining with Jesus and his disciples, for there were many who followed him. And the scribes of the Pharisees, when they saw that he was eating with sinners and tax collectors, said to his disciples, "Why does he eat with tax collectors and sinners?" And when Jesus heard it, he said to them, "Those who are well have no need of a physician, but those who are sick. I came not to call the righteous, but sinners." (Mark 2:15–17)

Jesus seeks out sinners because "[He] came into the world to save sinners" (1 Timothy 1:15b).

Jesus knows what it is to be tempted because He experienced it (Hebrews 4:15)! That awareness uniquely equips Him to be our advocate: "If anyone does sin, we have an advocate with the Father, Jesus Christ the righteous" (1 John 2:1b).

God's great love for sinners made THE way for us. "God shows his love for us in that while we were still sinners, Christ died for us" (Romans 5:8).

Sin is *not* a list of do's and don'ts. It begins with not treasuring God as He deserves to be treasured, which leads to sinful behaviors that further distort our view of God and diminish our appreciation of His authority over us.

"What is sin?" John Piper asks. His answer:

The glory of God not honored.
The holiness of God not reverenced.
The greatness of God not admired.
The power of God not praised.
The truth of God not sought.
The wisdom of God not esteemed.
The beauty of God not treasured.
The goodness of God not savored.
The faithfulness of God not trusted.
The promises of God not believed.
The commandments of God not obeyed.
The justice of God not respected.
The wrath of God not feared.
The grace of God not cherished.
The presence of God not prized.
The person of God not loved.

Hurt not your conscience with any known sin.
SAMUEL RUTHERFORD

I confess my iniquity; I am sorry for my sin.
PSALM 38:18

Your sins are forgiven for his name's sake.
1 JOHN 2:12b

In repentance, I am relieved of my sin by God's forgiveness.

God, my Father, is as eager to forgive me of my daily sins as He was to redeem me! My part is to confess any known sin and to scan my life for any hidden sin. Even in this, I need God's help; the Holy Spirit is my Helper—my Helper!—in rooting out my sin. "He will convict the world concerning sin. . . . He will guide you into all the truth" (John 16:8a, 13a).

That is all we need to do! It is simply all. When we confess it, we are forgiven of the sin that has clung so closely. We are released to walk in obedience!

I, like many protestants, didn't grow up with an emphasis on the need for regular confession of sin. When I was a child, I mistook the conviction of sin for the need of salvation. My parents were often chagrined to be notified by jubilant Sunday school teachers that I had just become a Christian—again! I didn't know that I didn't need another salvation, I just needed repentance.

With that in mind, this segment of *Prayer PathWay* is different than the others in that it provides step-by-step guidance. In addition to a thorough explanation of repentance, this section lists verses alphabetically by topic to help you as you seek out and confess sin and to equip you to fight sin, to relent, repent, receive, and resolve. Search your Bible to find additional help in each of these areas and far more.

In repentance, we are forgiven sinners. Our Good Shepherd has lain down His life for us. We can say with John Newton: "I am a great sinner and . . . Christ is a great Savior." We don't need to wallow in despair and in bondage; we are free.

The Bible is our most helpful guide and the Holy Spirit our most reliable teacher. By immersing ourselves in the Word of God, with the Spirit's help, we will find everything we need for life and godliness (2 Peter 1:3). He hasn't left us on our own to make our way.

Almighty God, unto whom all hearts be open, all desires known, and from whom no secrets are hid: Cleanse the thoughts of our hearts by the inspiration of Thy Holy Spirit, that we may perfectly love Thee, and worthily magnify Thy holy name; through Christ our Lord. Amen.

THE BOOK OF COMMON PRAYER

PATH MARKER

If your heart is heavy with sin, consider writing out a prayer of confession acknowledging your sin and accepting God's forgiveness.

RELENT, REPENT, RECEIVE, RESOLVE, REPEAT

GOD DESIRES THAT His children walk in obedience, but He makes a way for our forgiveness when we fail. *He makes the way!* Ponder what a gift that is—God gives us repentance. You can't do this for yourself—God has done it for you through Jesus.

> God exalted him at his right hand as Leader and Savior, to give repentance to Israel and forgiveness of sins. (Acts 5:31)

We need to stop on the path to search our lives for unconfessed sin. Sometimes, our sin is obvious to us because we feel guilty. But often we're oblivious to our sin—we need God to reveal it!

I suggest taking these steps: relent, repent, receive, and resolve.

1. RELENT OF ANY GRUDGES OR OFFENSES DONE TO YOU THAT HAVE SEPARATED YOU FROM OTHERS.

A first step in repentance is to think of anyone you need to forgive, even if that person hasn't asked for your forgiveness. Withholding grace doesn't give you more grace; it mutates into crippling bitterness. Grudges clutch at your soul; forgiving others weakens that hold. It frees you to move toward that person; it also means that God will forgive you what you ask of Him.

Releasing us from grudges seems to be a big priority for Jesus. He said, "Whenever you stand praying, forgive, if you have anything against anyone, so that your Father also who is in heaven may forgive you your trespasses" (Mark 11:25; also see Matthew 5:23–24; 6:15; 8:35).

Think of relenting as laying down an offense, putting it aside for now. You might not be able to fully or appropriately deal with the person or situation at this time, but you are freed of its control over you. You may need to revisit it when the time is ripe, but for now, relent.

Remember, forgiving others, while hard, is not optional; it is God's way. We have been forgiven; we *must* forgive.

The man who is truly forgiven and knows it, is a man who forgives.

DAVID MARTYN LLOYD-JONES

> Bearing with one another and, if one has a complaint against another, forgiving each other; as the Lord has forgiven you, so you also must forgive. (Colossians 3:13)

2. REPENT BY CONFESSING (ACTUALLY NAMING) THE SIN THAT YOU FEEL CONVICTED OF, IF YOU SINCERELY DESIRE TO TURN FROM IT.

If you think you don't have any sin to confess, you're lying to yourself (1 John 1:8), but you can't lie to God—He sees and He knows. "No creature is hidden from his sight, but all are naked and exposed to the eyes of him to whom we must give account" (Hebrews 4:13).

You have set our iniquities before you, our secret sins in the light of your presence.

PSALM 90:8

It's essential to know that any sin is, first and foremost, a sin against God. "Against you, you only, have I sinned and done what is evil in your sight" (Psalm 51:4a).

It's also essential to know that there is forgiveness on the other side of repentance: "If you, O Lord, should mark iniquities, O Lord, who could stand? But with you there is forgiveness, that you may be feared" (Psalm 130:3–4).

Ask God to show you what He sees in your heart and in your life. That is what you should confess: "Search me, O God, and know my heart! Try me and know my thoughts! And see if there be any grievous way in me, and lead me in the way everlasting!" (Psalm 139:23–24).

Jesus didn't give complicated instructions. He gave us clear commands to guide our behavior; those commands should also inform our confession and repentance: (1) "You shall love the Lord your God with all your heart and with all your soul and with all your mind and with all your strength" (Mark 12:30) and (2) "You shall love your neighbor as yourself" (Mark 12:31). That's it. It's *everything!*

The apostle Paul underscored those commands when he exhorted us to (1) "walk in a manner worthy of the calling to which you have been called" (Ephesians 4:1) and (2) to "[bear] with one another in love" (Ephesians 4:2).

Given the Bible's clear instructions, it would seem a simple thing to see our sin and repent of it. But the heart is deceitful, and we have blind spots. Make a habit of searching out your sin. The more time you spend in understanding your sin and in seeking repentance, the more sensitive you will become to anything that mars your relationship with God and hurts others.

Use these simple questions to help you pinpoint your sin.

A. Your heart and your behavior toward God

- Are you loving God with all your heart, soul, mind, and strength? (Mark 12:30)
- Are you walking in a manner worthy of Christ's call? (Ephesians 4:1)

B. Your heart and your behavior toward people

- Are you loving people as you love yourself? (Mark 12:31)
- Are you lovingly bearing with others? (Ephesians 4:2)

Every commandment or exhortation in the Bible fits into one or both of those categories.

Another way to evaluate your heart and your behavior is to ask, "Am I cherishing any person, possession, or activity more than I cherish God?"

We *know* what matters most to us. It's what we think about, what we protect, what we defend, what we spend our money and time on. *That* is

Table 3. Heart and Behavior toward God

HEART	SOUL
Purity: Am I guarding my heart, mind, and body?	*Holiness:* Am I fighting sin?
Treasure: What am I most valuing?	*Idolatry:* Am I putting anything or anybody in God's place?
Abiding: Am I continually resting in Christ?	*Humility:* Am I prideful?
MIND	**STRENGTH**
Thoughts: What am I feeding my mind?	*Self-Control:* Am I spiritually and physically disciplined?
Honesty: Have I been completely honest?	*Work:* Am I working at my tasks enthusiastically?
Devotional Life: Have I been devoted to the Word and to prayer?	*Body:* Am I keeping habits that are healthy for my physical body?

Table 4. Heart and Behavior toward People

Have I shown love?	Have I been boastful?	Have I been resentful?
Have I been patient?	Have I been arrogant?	Have I pointed others to God?
Have I been kind?	Have I insisted on having my own way?	
Have I been envious?		How have I used my tongue?
How have I expressed anger?	Have I been rude?	
	Have I been irritable?	Have I forgiven?

where our hearts are. Jesus said, "For where your treasure is, there will your heart be also" (Luke 12:34), and deep down we know it.

We *must* confess sin in order to be heard by God. "If I had cherished iniquity in my heart, the Lord would not have listened" (Psalm 66:18). He wants us to be *free* to cherish Him and His gifts.

Confession sounds like this:

> I confess my iniquity;
>> I am sorry for my sin. (Psalm 38:18)

> Do not forsake me, O LORD!
>> O my God, be not far from me!
> Make haste to help me,
>> O Lord, my salvation! (Psalm 38:21–22)

Being forgiven sounds like this:

> Your sins are forgiven for his name's sake. (1 John 2:12b)

> For I will be merciful toward their iniquities, and I will remember their sins no more. (Hebrews 8:12)

3. RECEIVE GOD'S FORGIVENESS.

In repentance, you have been honest about what God already knows. You have consciously turned from your sin and asked God to forgive you. You have been heard. You are forgiven—completely forgiven! *Your good God has done it again: He has forgiven sin.*

> If we confess our sins, he is faithful and just to forgive us our sins and to cleanse us from all unrighteousness. (1 John 1:9)

> He does not deal with us according to our sins,
>> nor repay us according to our iniquities.
> For as high as the heavens are above the earth,
>> so great is his steadfast love toward those who fear him;
> as far as the east is from the west,
>> so far does he remove our transgressions from us. (Psalm 103:10–12)

You were plagued with your sin (even if you ignored it, you were plagued and pursued and tormented by your sin). *Because of God's forgiveness, you are blessed!*

David explains this powerful reality:

Blessed is the one whose transgression is forgiven,
    whose sin is covered.
Blessed is the man against whom the LORD counts no iniquity,
    and in whose spirit there is no deceit.

For when I kept silent, my bones wasted away
    through my groaning all day long.
For day and night your hand was heavy upon me;
    my strength was dried up as by the heat of summer. Selah

I acknowledged my sin to you,
    and I did not cover my iniquity;
I said, "I will confess my transgressions to the LORD,"
    and you forgave the iniquity of my sin. Selah (Psalm 32:1-5)

Now, forgiven sinner, receive God's forgiveness!

And he said to her, "Your sins are forgiven." (Luke 7:48)

4. RESOLVE, WITH GOD'S HELP, TO STOP SINNING.

After you've been forgiven, you have new freedom and, often, new energy to walk in obedience. Resolve to daily fight sin.

God is with us as we walk His path of obedience. The Holy Spirit whispers the way! "Your ears shall hear a word behind you, saying, 'This is the way, walk in it,' when you turn to the right or when you turn to the left" (Isaiah 30:21).

And when alternate routes beckon us, God is there, providing an escape route: "No temptation has overtaken you that is not common to man. God is faithful, and he will not let you be tempted beyond your ability, but with the temptation he will also provide the way of escape, that you may be able to endure it" (1 Corinthians 10:13).

Fighting sin requires us to *resolve* to fight sin. It is a determined sense

not that I have already obtained this or am already perfect, but I press on to make it my own, because Christ Jesus has made me his own. Brothers, I do not consider that I have made it my own. But one thing I do: forgetting what lies behind and straining forward to what lies ahead, I press on toward the goal for the prize of the upward call of God in Christ Jesus. (Philippians 3:12–14)

It is the strengthening reality that we are not alone on this path. "Since we are surrounded by so great a cloud of witnesses, let us also lay aside every weight, and sin which clings so closely, and let us run with endurance the race that is set before us" (Hebrews 12:1).

Resolved, never to do anything, which I should be afraid to do, if it were the last hour of my life.

JONATHAN EDWARDS

To *resolve* is active, not passive. To live a life of resolve, we may need to ask for help, change our environment, adjust our habits, and sever relationships. Jesus says we must cut off anything—*anything*—that causes us to stumble in our lives of obedience (Matthew 5:29–30).

As John Owen reminds us, "you must always be killing sin or it will be killing you."

And Jesus simply and firmly says, "Go, and from now on sin no more" (John 8:11b).

Nothing in my hand I bring; simply to thy cross I cling.

AUGUSTUS TOPLADY

5. BUT WHAT DO YOU DO WHEN YOU SIN AGAIN? REPEAT!

God *knows* that we will sin again. He *knows*, and He is waiting to repeatedly forgive us!

The LORD is merciful and gracious,
  slow to anger and abounding in steadfast love.
He will not always chide,
  nor will he keep his anger forever.
He does not deal with us according to our sins,
  nor repay us according to our iniquities.
For as high as the heavens are above the earth,
  so great is his steadfast love toward those who fear him;
as far as the east is from the west,
  so far does he remove our transgressions from us.

As a father shows compassion to his children,
> so the LORD shows compassion to those who fear him.
For he knows our frame;
> he remembers that we are dust. (Psalm 103:8–14)

Run to God. He knows that you need Him. He is waiting for you. Relent again. Repent again. Receive again. Resolve again. We have a very patient God; He knows our weaknesses. We will always struggle with sin, but when we repent as soon as we are aware of our sin, it begins to lose its hold.

*Let me face what
Thou dost send
with the strength
Thou dost supply.*

JOHN BAILLIE

Across the centuries, Martin Luther reminds us: "We are not yet what we shall be, but we are growing toward it; the process is not yet finished but it is going on. This is not the end but it is the road; all does not yet gleam in glory but all is purified."

To this end we always pray for you, that our God may make you worthy of his calling and may fulfill every resolve for good and every work of faith by his power, so that the name of our Lord Jesus may be glorified in you, and you in him, according to the grace of our God and the Lord Jesus Christ. (2 Thessalonians 1:11–12)

Refer to Prayer Pointers (pp. 73–93) for verses that will help you discern and fight sin.

A Prayer of Repentance

Dear Forgiving Father, Sacrificed Savior, and Convicting Holy Spirit:

Who is a pardoning God like You? You have given us the gospel of salvation. You have redeemed us. And You hold out forgiveness for our daily sins.

Help me to see my sin as You do: sin that gently pricks my conscience but is easily ignored; sin that stabs in my heart and aches in my soul but feels like an essential part of me; sin that I hoard like a treasure instead of rejecting like poison; sin that I build and polish like an altar, not recognizing that it is an idol.

Do what You must to bring me to repentance. Then please see what Your Son has done on my behalf. *He Himself bore my sin in His body.* See Him and forgive me—and then strengthen me to go and sin no more.

Your grace has abounded more than my sin!

I am redeemed.

Amen.

"For your name's sake, O Lord, pardon my guilt, for it is great."
Psalm 25:11

PRAYER POINTERS

HAVE I BEEN **ABIDING IN CHRIST?**

Jesus said: "Abide in me, and I in you. As the branch cannot bear fruit by itself, unless it abides in the vine, neither can you, unless you abide in me.... As the Father has loved me, so have I loved you. Abide in my love. If you keep my commandments, you will abide in my love, just as I have kept my Father's commandments and abide in his love."
John 15:4, 9–10

No one who abides in him keeps on sinning; no one who keeps on sinning has either seen him or known him.
1 John 3:6

HAVE I BEEN SPIRITUALLY **ALERT?**

Be strong in the Lord and in the strength of his might. Put on the whole armor of God, that you may be able to stand against the schemes of the devil ... praying at all times in the Spirit, with all prayer and supplication. To that end keep alert with all perseverance, making supplication for all the saints.
Ephesians 6:10–11, 18

You are all children of light, children of the day. We are not of the night or of the darkness. So then let us not sleep, as others do, but let us keep awake and be sober.
1 Thessalonians 5:5–6

Nor prayer is made by
man alone,
The Holy Spirit pleads,
And Jesus, on the eternal
throne,
For sinners intercedes.

JAMES
MONTGOMERY

HOW HAVE I EXPRESSED **ANGER?**

Refrain from anger, and forsake wrath! Fret not yourself; it tends only to evil.
Psalm 37:8

Jesus said: "You have heard that it was said to those of old, 'You shall not murder; and whoever murders will be liable to judgment.' But I say to you that everyone who is angry with his brother will be liable to judgment; whoever insults his brother will be liable to the council; and whoever says, 'You fool!' will be liable to the hell of fire. So if you are offering your gift at the altar and there remember that your brother has something against you, leave your gift there before the altar and go. First be reconciled to your brother, and then come and offer your gift."
Matthew 5:21–24

Be angry and do not sin; do not let the sun go down on your anger, and give no opportunity to the devil.
Ephesians 4:26–27

HAVE I BEEN **ANXIOUS?**

Have I not commanded you? Be strong and courageous. Do not be frightened, and do not be dismayed, for the LORD your God is with you wherever you go.
Joshua 1:9

The Lord is at hand; do not be anxious about anything, but in everything by prayer and supplication with thanksgiving let your requests be made known to God.
Philippians 4:5b–6

Say over and over to yourself, "I am . . . wayward [and] foolish. But He loves me! I have disobeyed and grieved Him ten thousand times. But He loves me! . . . I do not love Him, I am even angry with Him! But He loves me!"

ELIZABETH PRENTISS

74

Rejoice in hope, be patient in tribulation, be constant in prayer.
Romans 12:12

[Cast] all your anxieties on him, because he cares for you.
1 Peter 5:7

HAVE I BEEN **CONTENT?**

I have learned in whatever situation I am to be content.
Philippians 4:11b

God will supply every need of yours according to his riches in glory in Christ Jesus.
Philippians 4:19

HAVE I BEEN HAVING REGULAR DEVOTIONS?

This Book of the Law shall not depart from your mouth, but you shall meditate on it day and night, so that you may be careful to do according to all that is written in it. For then you will make your way prosperous, and then you will have good success.
Joshua 1:8

Oh how I love your law! It is my meditation all the day.
Psalm 119:97

Jesus said: "It is written, 'Man shall not live by bread alone, but by every word that comes from the mouth of God.'"
Matthew 4:4

Let the word of Christ dwell in you richly.
Colossians 3:16a

Give us grace to repent every day for the sins of every day, so that when we come to die, we may have the sins but of one day to repent of, and so we may be continually easy.

ANDREW MURRAY

HAVE I BEEN AN **ENCOURAGER?**

The Lord GOD has given me the tongue of those who are taught, that I may know how to sustain with a word him who is weary.
Isaiah 50:4a

Admonish the idle, encourage the fainthearted, help the weak, be patient with them all.
1 Thessalonians 5:14

HOW HAVE I BEEN USING **FOOD?**

Man does not live by bread alone, but man lives by every word that comes from the mouth of the LORD.
Deuteronomy 8:3b

Jesus said: "My food is to do the will of him who sent me and to accomplish his work."
John 4:34

The kingdom of God is not a matter of eating and drinking but of righteousness and peace and joy in the Holy Spirit.
Romans 14:17

So, whether you eat or drink, or whatever you do, do all to the glory of God.
1 Corinthians 10:31

HAVE I BEEN **FORGIVING?**

Jesus said: "For if you forgive others their trespasses, your heavenly Father will also forgive you,

Pardon all my sins, known and unknown, felt and unfelt, confessed and not confessed, remembered or forgotten.

THE VALLEY OF VISION

but if you do not forgive others their trespasses, neither will your Father forgive your trespasses."
Matthew 6:14–15

Peter . . . said to him, "Lord, how often will my brother sin against me, and I forgive him? As many as seven times?" Jesus said to him, "I do not say to you seven times, but seventy-seven times."
Matthew 18:21–22

Be kind to one another, tenderhearted, forgiving one another, as God in Christ forgave you.
Ephesians 4:32

[Bear] with one another and, if one has a complaint against another, forgiving each other; as the Lord has forgiven you, so you also must forgive.
Colossians 3:13

WHAT KIND OF **FRIENDS** DO I HAVE?

Whoever walks with the wise becomes wise, but the companion of fools will suffer harm.
Proverbs 13:20

Make no friendship with a man given to anger.
Proverbs 22:24a

Be not among drunkards or among gluttonous eaters of meat, for the drunkard and the glutton will come to poverty, and slumber will clothe them with rags.
Proverbs 23:20–21

Take heed of little sins.
JOHN BUNYAN

Sin lived in makes the heart hard and God's ear deaf. . . . It is foolish to pray against sin and then to sin against prayer.
THOMAS WATSON

HAVE I BEEN **GENEROUS** WITH WHAT GOD HAS GIVEN ME?

If you pour yourself out for the hungry and satisfy the desire of the afflicted, then shall your light rise in the darkness and your gloom be as the noonday.
Isaiah 58:10

Do not neglect to do good and to share what you have, for such sacrifices are pleasing to God.
Hebrews 13:16

HAVE I BEEN **GRUMBLING?**

Better is a dry morsel with quiet than a house full of feasting with strife.
Proverbs 17:1

Do all things without grumbling or disputing, that you may be blameless and innocent, children of God without blemish in the midst of a crooked and twisted generation, among whom you shine as lights in the world.
Philippians 2:14–15

I have learned in whatever situation I am to be content. I know how to be brought low, and I know how to abound. In any and every circumstance, I have learned the secret of facing plenty and hunger, abundance and need.
Philippians 4:11b–12

Show hospitality to one another without grumbling.
1 Peter 4:9

Anyone who would have power in prayer must be merciless in dealing with his own sins.

R.A. TORREY

HAVE I BEEN STRIVING TO BE HOLY?

You shall be holy, for I the LORD your God am holy.
Leviticus 19:2b

Do you not know that you are God's temple and
that God's Spirit dwells in you? If anyone destroys
God's temple, God will destroy him. For God's
temple is holy, and you are that temple.
1 Corinthians 3:16–17

Abstain from every form of evil.
1 Thessalonians 5:22

Let everyone who names the name of the Lord
depart from iniquity.
2 Timothy 2:19b

As obedient children, do not be conformed to the passions of your former ignorance, but as he who called
you is holy, you also be holy in all your conduct,
since it is written, "You shall be holy, for I am holy."
1 Peter 1:14–16

HAVE I BEEN HONEST?

Truthful lips endure forever, but a lying tongue is
but for a moment.
Proverbs 12:19

The getting of treasures by a lying tongue is a fleeting vapor and a snare of death.
Proverbs 21:6

Do not lie to one another.
Colossians 3:9a

*How little people know
who think that holiness
is dull. . . . When one
meets the real thing, it's
irresistible.*

C.S. LEWIS

DO I HAVE ANY **IDOLS** (PEOPLE, THINGS, OR BEHAVIORS THAT I CLING TO WHEN I SHOULD CLING TO GOD)?

Let your heart . . . be wholly true to the Lord our God, walking in his statutes and keeping his commandments.
1 Kings 8:61a

Flee from idolatry.
1 Corinthians 10:14b

Put to death therefore what is earthly in you: sexual immorality, impurity, passion, evil desire, and covetousness, which is idolatry.
Colossians 3:5

Little children, keep yourselves from idols.
1 John 5:21

HAVE I BEEN **JEALOUS?**

The getting of treasures by a lying tongue is a fleeting vapor and a snare of death.
Proverbs 21:6

Let not your heart envy sinners, but continue in the fear of the LORD all the day.
Proverbs 23:17

Jesus said: "Take care, and be on your guard against all covetousness, for one's life does not consist in the abundance of his possessions."
Luke 12:15

The truth is that while Christ dwells in the believer's new nature, He has strong competition from the believer's old nature. The warfare between the old and the new goes on.

A. W. TOZER

HAVE I BEEN **LOVING?**

Jesus said: "Love your enemies, do good to those who hate you, bless those who curse you, pray for those who abuse you."
Luke 6:27b–28

Love is patient and kind; love does not envy or boast; it is not arrogant or rude. It does not insist on its own way; it is not irritable or resentful; it does not rejoice at wrongdoing, but rejoices with the truth. Love bears all things, believes all things, hopes all things, endures all things. Love never ends.
1 Corinthians 13:4–8a

Above all, keep loving one another earnestly, since love covers a multitude of sins.
1 Peter 4:8

Little children, let us not love in word or talk but in deed and in truth.
1 John 3:18

Anyone who does not love does not know God, because God is love.
1 John 4:8

WHAT HAVE I BEEN DOING WITH MY **MONEY?**

If riches increase, set not your heart on them.
Psalm 62:10b

In confession the light of the Gospel breaks into the darkness and seclusion of the heart. The sin must be brought into the light.

DIETRICH
BONHOEFFER

Jesus said "No one can serve two masters, for either he will hate the one and love the other, or he will be devoted to the one and despise the other. You cannot serve God and money."
Matthew 6:24

Keep your life free from love of money, and be content with what you have, for he has said, "I will never leave you nor forsake you."
Hebrews 13:5

HAVE I BEEN **OBEDIENT?**

Jesus said: "If anyone would come after me, let him deny himself and take up his cross and follow me. For whoever would save his life will lose it, but whoever loses his life for my sake will find it."
Matthew 16:24b–25

Whoever keeps his commandments abides in God, and God in him.
1 John 3:24a

By this we know that we love the children of God, when we love God and obey his commandments. For this is the love of God, that we keep his commandments. And his commandments are not burdensome.
1 John 5:2–3

HAVE I BEEN **PATIENT?**

Love is patient and kind.
1 Corinthians 13:4a

Our sins are like a wall between us and God, which prevents him from hearing our prayers.
JOHN CALVIN

We urge you, brothers, admonish the idle, encourage the fainthearted, help the weak, be patient with them all.
1 Thessalonians 5:14

HAVE I BEEN A PEACEMAKER?

Jesus said: "Blessed are the peacemakers, for they shall be called sons of God."
Matthew 5:9

Live in harmony with one another.
Romans 12:16a

Strive for peace with everyone, and for the holiness without which no one will see the Lord.
Hebrews 12:14

HAVE I BEEN PRAYING?

Moreover, as for me, far be it from me that I should sin against the LORD by ceasing to pray for you.
1 Samuel 12:23a

Jesus said: "Watch and pray that you may not enter into temptation. The spirit indeed is willing, but the flesh is weak."
Matthew 26:41

Continue steadfastly in prayer, being watchful in it with thanksgiving.
Colossians 4:2

Rejoice always, pray without ceasing, give thanks in all circumstances; for this is the will of God in Christ Jesus for you.
1 Thessalonians 5:16–18

But really the habit of unceasing prayer does not require time. It is but looking into God's face and saying, "Help me in this." "Bless me as I do this."

J. R. MILLER

HAVE I BEEN PROUD?

Jesus said: "Beware of practicing your righteousness before other people in order to be seen by them, for then you will have no reward from your Father who is in heaven."
Matthew 6:1

Jesus said: "Judge not, that you be not judged. For with the judgment you pronounce you will be judged, and with the measure you use it will be measured to you. Why do you see the speck that is in your brother's eye, but do not notice the log that is in your own eye?"
Matthew 7:1–3

Do nothing from selfish ambition or conceit, but in humility count others more significant than yourselves. Let each of you look not only to his own interests, but also to the interests of others.
Philippians 2:3–4

God opposes the proud, but gives grace to the humble.
James 4:6b

HAVE I BEEN STRIVING TO BE PURE?

I will not set before my eyes anything that is worthless. . . . A perverse heart shall be far from me; I will know nothing of evil.
Psalm 101:3–4

Till sin be bitter, Christ will not be sweet.
THOMAS WATSON

How can a young man keep his way pure? By guarding it according to your word. With my whole heart I seek you; let me not wander from

your commandments! I have stored up your word in my heart, that I might not sin against you.
Psalm 119:9–11

Jesus said: "Blessed are the pure in heart, for they shall see God."
Matthew 5:8

Jesus said: "Go, and from now on sin no more."
John 8:11b

Flee from sexual immorality. Every other sin a person commits is outside the body, but the sexually immoral person sins against his own body. Or do you not know that your body is a temple of the Holy Spirit within you, whom you have from God? You are not your own, for you were bought with a price. So glorify God in your body.
1 Corinthians 6:18–20

Not that I have already obtained this or am already perfect, but I press on to make it my own, because Christ Jesus has made me his own. Brothers, I do not consider that I have made it my own. But one thing I do: forgetting what lies behind and straining forward to what lies ahead, I press on toward the goal for the prize of the upward call of God in Christ Jesus.
Philippians 3:12–14

Since we are surrounded by so great a cloud of witnesses, let us also lay aside every weight, and sin which clings so closely, and let us run with endurance the race that is set before us.
Hebrews 12:1

Oh, you don't know what a great sinner I am; but Christ's love is greater still.

ELIZABETH
PRENTISS

Put away all filthiness and rampant wickedness and receive with meekness the implanted word, which is able to save your souls.
James 1:21

Be diligent to be found by him without spot or blemish, and at peace.
2 Peter 3:14b

HAVE I BEEN **RESPECTFUL?**

Obey your leaders and submit to them, for they are keeping watch over your souls, as those who will have to give an account. Let them do this with joy and not with groaning, for that would be of no advantage to you.
Hebrews 13:17

Honor everyone. Love the brotherhood. Fear God. Honor the emperor.
1 Peter 2:17

HAVE I HAD **SELF-CONTROL** OVER MY BODY AND MIND?

I hold back my feet from every evil way, in order to keep your word.
Psalm 119:101

Our Great Father does not wait for us to be good and wise to love us, but loves us, and loves to help us in the very thick of our struggles with folly and sin.

JULIANA H. EWING

Present your bodies as a living sacrifice, holy and acceptable to God, which is your spiritual worship. Do not be conformed to this world, but be transformed by the renewal of your mind, that by testing you may discern what is the will of God, what is good and acceptable and perfect.
Romans 12:1b–2

Do you not know that you are God's temple and that God's Spirit dwells in you? If anyone destroys God's temple, God will destroy him. For God's temple is holy, and you are that temple.

1 Corinthians 3:16–17

Wake up from your drunken stupor, as is right, and do not go on sinning.

1 Corinthians 15:34a

For the grace of God has appeared, bringing salvation for all people, training us to renounce ungodliness and worldly passions, and to live self-controlled, upright, and godly lives in the present age.

Titus 2:11–12

HAVE I BEEN A **SERVANT**?

Jesus said: "Whoever would be great among you must be your servant, and whoever would be first among you must be slave of all. For even the Son of Man came not to be served but to serve, and to give his life as a ransom for many."

Mark 10:43b–45

Let each of you look not only to his own interests, but also to the interests of others.

Philippians 2:4

HAVE I BEEN **TEACHABLE**?

Teach me your way, O LORD, that I may walk in your truth; unite my heart to fear your name.

Psalm 86:11

To get up every morning with the firm resolve to find pleasure in those duties, and do them well, and finish the work which God has given us to do, that is to drink Christ's cup. The humblest occupation has in it materials of discipline for the highest heaven.

FREDERICK W. ROBERTSON

Whoever loves discipline loves knowledge, but he who hates reproof is stupid.

Proverbs 12:1

Whoever ignores instruction despises himself, but he who listens to reproof gains intelligence. The fear of the LORD is instruction in wisdom, and humility comes before honor.

Proverbs 15:32–33

HAVE I FOUGHT TEMPTATION?

No temptation has overtaken you that is not common to man. God is faithful, and he will not let you be tempted beyond your ability, but with the temptation he will also provide the way of escape, that you may be able to endure it.

1 Corinthians 10:13

For freedom Christ has set us free; stand firm therefore, and do not submit again to a yoke of slavery.

Galatians 5:1

HAVE I BEEN GUARDING MY THOUGHTS?

I will meditate on your precepts and fix my eyes on your ways. I will delight in your statutes; I will not forget your word.

Psalm 119:15–16

Whatever is true, whatever is honorable, whatever is just, whatever is pure, whatever is lovely, whatever is commendable, if there is any excellence, if there is anything worthy of praise, think about these things.

Philippians 4:8

Life requires countless "little deaths"— occasions when we are given the chance to say no to self and yes to God.

ELISABETH ELLIOT

Temptation is not a sin; it is a call to battle.

ERWIN W. LUTZER

See to it that no one takes you captive by philosophy and empty deceit, according to human tradition, according to the elemental spirits of the world, and not according to Christ.
Colossians 2:8

If then you have been raised with Christ, seek the things that are above, where Christ is, seated at the right hand of God. Set your minds on things that are above, not on things that are on earth. For you have died, and your life is hidden with Christ in God.
Colossians 3:1–3

HAVE I BEEN USING MY **TONGUE** IN A HURTFUL WAY?

Let the words of my mouth and the meditation of my heart be acceptable in your sight, O LORD, my rock and my redeemer.
Psalm 19:14

Set a guard, O LORD, over my mouth; keep watch over the door of my lips!
Psalm 141:3

When words are many, transgression is not lacking, but whoever restrains his lips is prudent.
Proverbs 10:19

Let there be no filthiness nor foolish talk nor crude joking, which are out of place, but instead let there be thanksgiving.
Ephesians 5:4

Be quick to hear, slow to speak, slow to anger.
James 1:19b

To accept Christ it is necessary that we reject what is contrary to Him.
A. W. TOZER

WHAT HAVE I BEEN **TREASURING**?

Delight yourself in the LORD, and he will give you
the desires of your heart.
Psalm 37:4

Jesus said: "Do not lay up for yourselves treasures
on earth. . . . For where your treasure is, there your
heart will be also."
Matthew 6:19a, 21

Do not love the world or the things in the world.
If anyone loves the world, the love of the Father
is not in him. For all that is in the world—the
desires of the flesh and the desires of the eyes and
pride of life—is not from the Father but is from
the world. And the world is passing away along
with its desires, but whoever does the will of God
abides forever.
1 John 2:15–17

HAVE I BEEN DOING MY **WORK** IN A WAY THAT HONORS GOD?

Jesus said: "Do not work for the food that perishes, but for the food that endures to eternal life,
which the Son of Man will give to you. For on
him God the Father has set his seal."
John 6:27

Whatever you do, work heartily, as for the Lord
and not for men.
Colossians 3:23

*There is not a square inch
in the whole domain of
our human existence
over which Christ, who
is Sovereign over all, does
not cry: "Mine!"*

ABRAHAM KUYPER

FOR MEN:

Be strong, and show yourself a man, and keep the charge of the LORD your God, walking in his ways and keeping his statutes, his commandments, his rules.

1 Kings 2:2b–3a

Fathers, do not provoke your children to anger, but bring them up in the discipline and instruction of the Lord.

Ephesians 6:4

Husbands, love your wives, and do not be harsh with them.

Colossians 3:19

Fathers, do not provoke your children, lest they become discouraged.

Colossians 3:21

Husbands, live with your wives in an understanding way, showing honor to the woman as the weaker vessel, since they are heirs with you of the grace of life, so that your prayers may not be hindered.

1 Peter 3:7

FOR WOMEN:

The wisest of women builds her house, but folly with her own hands tears it down.

Proverbs 14:1

She does him good, and not harm, all the days of her life.

Proverbs 31:12

Teach me the happy art of attending to things temporal with a mind intent on things eternal.

THE VALLEY OF VISION

She opens her mouth with wisdom, and the teaching of kindness is on her tongue.
Proverbs 31:26

She looks well to the ways of her household and does not eat the bread of idleness.
Proverbs 31:27

Let the wife see that she respects her husband.
Ephesians 5:33b

Wives, submit to your husbands, as is fitting in the Lord.
Colossians 3:18

Women should adorn themselves in respectable apparel, with modesty and self-control.
1 Timothy 2:9

Do not let your adorning be external—the braiding of hair and the putting on of gold jewelry, or the clothing you wear—but let your adorning be the hidden person of the heart with the imperishable beauty of a gentle and quiet spirit, which in God's sight is very precious. For this is how the holy women who hoped in God used to adorn themselves, by submitting to their own husbands.
1 Peter 3:3–5

FOR CHILDREN:

Behold, how good and pleasant it is when brothers dwell in unity!
Psalm 133:1

In the old days this sound advice was given to the bride: "My dear, make your husband glad to cross his threshold at night"; and to the groom, "Make your wife sorry to have you leave."

MARTIN LUTHER

Children, obey your parents in the Lord, for this
is right.
Ephesians 6:1

Children, obey your parents in everything, for
this pleases the Lord.
Colossians 3:20

Let no one despise you for your youth, but set the
believers an example in speech, in conduct, in love,
in faith, in purity.
1 Timothy 4:12

*To be entirely safe from
the devil's snares the man
of God must be completely
obedient to the Word of
the Lord.*

A. W. TOZER

Additional Verses

Additional Verses

Additional Verses

PRAISE

REPENT

ASK

YIELD

EXPRESS THANKS

REJOICE

SHALOM.

Do not be anxious about anything,
but in everything
by prayer and supplication
with thanksgiving
let your requests
be made known to God.

PHILIPPIANS 4:6

Prayer is not overcoming
God's reluctance,
but laying hold of
His highest willingness.

RICHARD CHENEVIX
TRENCH

ASK

God Provides

As our good Father, God is eager to have His children turn to Him; to ask Him for things that concern us. Most of the passages in the Bible that have to do with asking have a needy or desperate tone—cries for help, forgiveness, refuge, protection, wisdom, justice, and rest.

- David prayed for his people: "O Lord, the God of Abraham, Isaac, and Israel, our fathers, keep forever such purposes and thoughts in the hearts of your people, and direct their hearts toward you" (1 Chronicles 29:18).
- The psalmist prayed for help: "In my distress I called to the Lord, and he answered me" (Psalm 120:1).
- The psalmist prayed for deliverance: "Call upon me in the day of trouble; I will deliver you, and you shall glorify me." (Psalm 50:15)

    Before they call I will answer; while they are yet speaking I will hear.

    ISAIAH 65:24

- The author of Lamentations cried out for God to listen: "I called on your name, O Lord, from the depths of the pit; you heard my plea, 'Do not close your ear to my cry for help!' You came near when I called on you; you said, 'Do not fear!'" (Lamentations 3:55–57).
- In Jesus' parable in Luke 18, a persistent, desperate widow asking for justice received it. Jesus said, "Will not God give justice to his elect,

who cry to him day and night? Will he delay long over them? I tell you, he will give justice to them speedily" (Luke 18:7–8a).

• Paul and Timothy prayed for the spiritual health of the Colossians: "We have not ceased to pray for you, asking that you may be filled with the knowledge of his will in all spiritual wisdom and understanding, so as to walk in a manner worthy of the Lord" (Colossians 1:9b–10a).

I will help you. It is a small thing for me, your God, to help you. Consider what I have already done. What! Not help you! I died for you. Since I have done the greater, will I not do less? Your requests are nothing compared with what I am willing to give. You need much, but it is nothing for me to grant your needs. Help you? Fear not! I will help you.

CHARLES HADDON SPURGEON

Numerous times in the Gospels, Jesus goes away, alone to pray. We don't know what He prayed about, but we do know that sometimes He prayed all night. We have this powerful image from the author of Hebrews: "Jesus offered up prayers and supplications, with loud cries and tears, to him who was able to save him from death, and he was heard because of his reverence" (Hebrews 5:7).

The night before He died, Jesus prayed for *us*:

I am praying for them. I am not praying for the world but for those whom you have given me, for they are yours. All mine are yours, and yours are mine, and I am glorified in them. And I am no longer in the world, but they are in the world, and I am coming to you. Holy Father, keep them in your name. . . . I do not ask that you take them out of the world, but that you keep them from the evil one. They are not of the world, just as I am not of the world. Sanctify them in the truth; your word is truth. (John 17:9–17)

Jesus—the Savior of the world—prayed for us, two thousand years ago, as He faced His imminent and painful death. This reality needs to settle on us: Jesus prayed for us.

And now? He is *still* praying for us. He is living to make continual intercession for us (Romans 8:34, Hebrews 7:25). Always! And, according to Romans 8:26–27, the Holy Spirit prays for us more passionately than we can pray for ourselves.

That knowledge should affect how we pray—what we ask for and how we ask.

First, I ask: Is what I'm requesting for His glory and for my good? Am I seeking to align my will to God's will? I know that I am when I'm asking for wisdom or holiness or strength against temptation or for the souls of the

I have lived to thank God that all my prayers have not been answered.

JEAN INGELOW

lost—or anything else we've been commanded to pray about. But what about praying for my personal longings and desires, wants and needs, large and small? I can still request with humble boldness, yielding my will to His, trusting that my good Father knows better than I do what is best for me.

According to Paul, it appears that the antidote for anxiety about anything is asking: "Do not be anxious about anything, but in everything by prayer and supplication with thanksgiving let your requests be made known to God." (Philippians 4:6)

In addition to praying for our own needs, we're also to pray for others—as Jesus intercedes for us, we are to intercede for others. This kind of praying is close to God's heart. We're told to pray for those who persecute us (Matthew 5:44), for leaders (1 Timothy 2:2), for our enemies (Luke 6:27–28), for the city (Jeremiah 29:7), for the sick (James 5:14), for the unsaved (Romans 10:1), for missionaries (Matthew 9:38), and for all people (1 Timothy 2:1).

Andrew Murray exhorts: "Let us each find out what the work is, and which souls are entrusted to our special prayers; let us make intercession for them our life of fellowship with God." Which souls are entrusted to me? What an honor and calling it is to pray for someone for whom, perhaps, no one else is praying.

This testimony, from the life of George Mueller has fueled my interceding:

Intercession means no more than to bring our brother into the presence of God, to see him under the Cross of Jesus as a poor human being and sinner in need of grace.

DIETRICH BONHOEFFER

One day George Mueller began praying for five of his friends. After many months, one of them came to the Lord. Ten years later, two others were converted. It took 25 years before the fourth man was saved.

Mueller persevered in prayer until his death for the fifth friend, and throughout those 52 years he never gave up hoping that he would accept Christ! His faith was rewarded, for soon after Mueller's funeral the last one was saved.[1]

We can ask freely when our prayers are moored to truths like:

- "No good thing does he withhold from those who walk uprightly" (Psalm 84:11b).
- "His divine power has granted to us all things that pertain to life and godliness" (2 Peter 1:3a).
- "My God will supply every need of yours according to his riches in glory in Christ Jesus" (Philippians 4:19).

Jesus said to him, "'If you can'! All things are possible for one who believes." Immediately the father of the child cried out and said, "I believe; help my unbelief!"

MARK 9:23–24

To ask is *not* to demand. It is to humbly and expectantly tell God what He already knows: my needs and my wants. It is to acknowledge Him as the Source. I wait patiently, trusting that God has great goodness in mind for me!

PATH MARKER
Consider starting a George Mueller prayer list. Ask God to show you the people you should pray for—the people for whom no one else is praying.

1. David Whyte III, *The Prayer Motivator* (Dallas: Torch Legacy Publications, 2010), 25.

A Prayer of Asking

Dear Generous Father, Miracle-working Master, and Over-flowing Holy Spirit:

I long to be so Godward in my desires that my requests align with Your great heart for people, possessions, passions, pursuits. May I ask eagerly as Your expectant child for *all that pertains to life and godliness*. May I request humbly for the journey of Your other sojourners. May I beg boldly for the redemption of Your lost lambs. May I weep persistently for the restoration of Your wandering ones. *Your purposes cannot be thwarted*. I am honored to pray into Your plans.

I am blessed.

Amen.

"I know that you can do all things, and that no purpose of yours can be thwarted."
Job 42:2

PRAYER PASSAGES

Moreover, as for me, far be it from me that I should sin against the LORD by ceasing to pray for you, and I will instruct you in the good and the right way. Only fear the LORD and serve him faithfully with all your heart. For consider what great things he has done for you.
1 Samuel 12:23–24

Yet have regard to the prayer of your servant and to his plea, O LORD my God, listening to the cry and to the prayer that your servant prays before you this day.
1 Kings 8:28

For you know your servant. . . . Therefore your servant has found courage to pray before you.
1 Chronicles 17:18b, 25b

So we fasted and implored our God for this, and he listened to our entreaty.
Ezra 8:23

O LORD God of heaven, the great and awesome God who keeps covenant and steadfast love with those who love him and keep his commandments, let your ear be attentive and your eyes open, to hear the prayer of your servant.
Nehemiah 1:5–6a

I know that you can do all things, and that no purpose of yours can be thwarted.
Job 42:2

*O Lord, I do not pray
for tasks equal to my
strength: I ask for
strength equal to my tasks.*
PHILLIPS BROOKS

*Turn your eyes upon Jesus,
Look full in His wonderful
face,
And the things of earth
will grow strangely dim,
In the light of His glory
and grace.*
HELEN H. LEMMEL

Answer me when I call, O God of my righteousness! You have given me relief when I was in distress. Be gracious to me and hear my prayer! . . . But know that the Lord has set apart the godly for himself; the Lord hears when I call to him.
Psalm 4:1, 3

Give ear to my words, O LORD; consider my groaning. Give attention to the sound of my cry, my King and my God, for to you do I pray.
Psalm 5:1–2

The LORD has heard my plea; the LORD accepts my prayer.
Psalm 6:9

O LORD, you hear the desire of the afflicted; you will strengthen their heart; you will incline your ear.
Psalm 10:17

May he grant you your heart's desire and fulfill all your plans! May we shout for joy over your salvation, and in the name of our God set up our banners! May the LORD fulfill all your petitions!
Psalm 20:4–5

Hear, O LORD, when I cry aloud; be gracious to me and answer me!
Psalm 27:7

Call upon me in the day of trouble; I will deliver you, and you shall glorify me.
Psalm 50:15

O God, hear my prayer; give ear to the words of my mouth.
Psalm 54:2

O Father, thou art enthroned to hear my prayers, O Jesus, thy hand is outstretched to take my petitions,
O Holy Spirit, thou art willing to help my infirmities, to show me my need, to supply words, to pray within me, to strengthen me that I faint not in supplication.
O Triune God, who commandeth the universe, thou has commended me to ask for those things that concern thy kingdom and my soul.

THE VALLEY OF VISION

But as for me, my prayer is to you, O Lord. At an acceptable time, O God, in the abundance of your steadfast love answer me in your saving faithfulness. . . . Answer me, O Lord, for your steadfast love is good; according to your abundant mercy, turn to me.
Psalm 69:13, 16

I cry aloud to God, aloud to God, and he will hear me.
Psalm 77:1

Give ear, O Lord, to my prayer; listen to my plea for grace. In the day of my trouble I call upon you, for you answer me.
Psalm 86:6–7

O Lord, God of my salvation; I cry out day and night before you. Let my prayer come before you; incline your ear to my cry!
Psalm 88:1–2

When he calls to me, I will answer him;
I will be with him in trouble; I will rescue him and honor him.
Psalm 91:15

I love the Lord, because he has heard my voice and my pleas for mercy. Because he inclined his ear to me, therefore I will call on him as long as I live.
Psalm 116:1–2

May He give us a large and strong heart to believe what mighty influence our prayers can exert.

ANDREW MURRAY

Deal bountifully with your servant, that I may live and keep your word. Open my eyes, that I may behold wondrous things out of your law. I am a sojourner on the earth.
Psalm 119:17–19a

In my distress I called to the LORD, and he answered me.
Psalm 120:1

On the day I called, you answered me; my strength of soul you increased.
Psalm 138:3

Hear my prayer, O LORD; give ear to my pleas for mercy! In your faithfulness answer me, in your righteousness!
Psalm 143:1

Before they call I will answer; while they are yet speaking I will hear.
Isaiah 65:24

I called on your name, O LORD, from the depths of the pit; you heard my plea, "Do not close your ear to my cry for help!" You came near when I called on you; you said, "Do not fear!" You have taken up my cause, O Lord; you have redeemed my life.
Lamentations 3:55–58

Therefore do not be anxious, saying, "What shall we eat?" or "What shall we drink?" or "What shall we wear?" For the Gentiles seek after all these things, and your heavenly Father knows that you need them all. But seek first the kingdom of God and his righteousness, and all these things will be added to you. Therefore do not be anxious about tomorrow, for tomorrow will be anxious for itself. Sufficient for the day is its own trouble.
Matthew 6:31–34

Earnest intercession will be sure to bring love with it. I do not believe you can hate a man for whom you habitually pray. If you dislike any brother Christian, pray for him doubly, not only for his sake, but for your own, that you may be cured of prejudice and saved from all unkind feeling.

CHARLES HADDON SPURGEON

Ask, and it will be given to you; seek, and you will find; knock, and it will be opened to you. For everyone who asks receives, and the one who seeks finds, and to the one who knocks it will be opened. Or which one of you, if his son asks him for bread, will give him a stone? Or if he asks for a fish, will give him a serpent? If you then, who are evil, know how to give good gifts to your children, how much more will your Father who is in heaven give good things to those who ask him!
Matthew 7:7–11

Then he said to his disciples, "The harvest is plentiful, but the laborers are few; therefore pray earnestly to the Lord of the harvest to send out laborers into his harvest."
Matthew 9:37–38

Again I say to you, if two of you agree on earth about anything they ask, it will be done for them by my Father in heaven. For where two or three are gathered in my name, there am I among them.
Matthew 18:19–20

Jesus looked at them and said, "With man this is impossible, but with God all things are possible."
Matthew 19:26

Jesus said to him . . . "All things are possible for one who believes." Immediately the father of the child cried out and said, "I believe; help my unbelief!"
Mark 9:23–24

Therefore I tell you, whatever you ask in prayer, believe that you have received it, and it will be yours. And whenever you stand praying, forgive,

This is believing indeed; the rolling all our desires and burdens over upon an almighty God; and where this is, it cannot choose but establish the heart in the midst of troubles and give it a calm within in the midst of the greatest storms.

ROBERT LEIGHTON

if you have anything against anyone, so that your Father also who is in heaven may forgive you your trespasses.
Mark 11:24–25

For nothing will be impossible with God.
Luke 1:37

And he said to his disciples, "Therefore I tell you, do not be anxious about your life, what you will eat, nor about your body, what you will put on. For life is more than food, and the body more than clothing."
Luke 12:22–23

[Jesus said:] Fear not, little flock, for it is your Father's good pleasure to give you the kingdom.
Luke 12:32

[Jesus said:] For where your treasure is, there will your heart be also.
Luke 12:34

[Jesus] told them a parable to the effect that they ought always to pray and not lose heart.
Luke 18:1

[Jesus said:] Whatever you ask in my name, this I will do, that the Father may be glorified in the Son. If you ask me anything in my name, I will do it.
John 14:13–14

[Jesus said:] If you abide in me, and my words abide in you, ask whatever you wish, and it will be done for you.
John 15:7

Lord, make me an instrument of Thy peace, Where there is hatred, let me sow love; where there is injury, pardon; where there is doubt, faith; where there is despair, hope; where there is darkness, light; where there is sadness, joy; O Divine Master, grant that I may not so much seek to be consoled as to console; to be understood as to understand; to be loved as to love. For it is in giving that we receive; it is in pardoning that we are pardoned; and it is in dying that we are born to eternal life.
PEACE PRAYER

[Jesus said:] Until now you have asked nothing in my name. Ask, and you will receive, that your joy may be full.

John 16:24

Bear one another's burdens, and so fulfill the law of Christ.

Galatians 6:2

For this reason I bow my knees before the Father, from whom every family in heaven and on earth is named, that according to the riches of his glory he may grant you to be strengthened with power through his Spirit in your inner being, so that Christ may dwell in your hearts through faith—that you, being rooted and grounded in love, may have strength to comprehend with all the saints what is the breadth and length and height and depth, and to know the love of Christ that surpasses knowledge, that you may be filled with all the fullness of God.

Ephesians 3:14–19

Now to him who is able to do far more abundantly than all that we ask or think, according to the power at work within us, to him be glory in the church and in Christ Jesus throughout all generations, forever and ever. Amen.

Ephesians 3:20–21

Praying at all times in the Spirit, with all prayer and supplication. To that end keep alert with all perseverance, making supplication for all the saints.

Ephesians 6:18

Do not be anxious about anything, but in every-thing by prayer and supplication with thanksgiv-

That which I know not, teach Thou me, O Lord, my God.

AMY CARMICHAEL

God will not delay one moment longer than is absolutely necessary; He will do all in His power to hasten and speed the answer.

ANDREW MURRAY

ing let your requests be made known to God. And the peace of God, which surpasses all understanding, will guard your hearts and your minds in Christ Jesus.

Philippians 4:6–7

And so, from the day we heard, we have not ceased to pray for you, asking that you may be filled with the knowledge of his will in all spiritual wisdom and understanding, so as to walk in a manner worthy of the Lord, fully pleasing to him, bearing fruit in every good work and increasing in the knowledge of God. May you be strengthened with all power, according to his glorious might, for all endurance and patience with joy, giving thanks to the Father, who has qualified you to share in the inheritance of the saints in light. He has delivered us from the domain of darkness and transferred us to the kingdom of his beloved Son, in whom we have redemption, the forgiveness of sins.

Colossians 1:9–14

To this end we always pray for you, that our God may make you worthy of his calling and may fulfill every resolve for good and every work of faith by his power, so that the name of our Lord Jesus may be glorified in you, and you in him, according to the grace of our God and the Lord Jesus Christ.

2 Thessalonians 1:11–12

First of all, then, I urge that supplications, prayers, intercessions, and thanksgivings be made for all people, for kings and all who are in high positions, that we may lead a peaceful and quiet life, godly and dignified in every way.

1 Timothy 2:1–2

We shall oppose both men and the devil if we maintain ourselves in prayer and if we persist in it. For we know that when a Christian prays in this way: "Dear Father, Your will be done," God replies to him, "Dear child, yes, it will be done inspite of the devil and the whole world."

MARTIN LUTHER

Let us then with confidence draw near to the throne of grace, that we may receive mercy and find grace to help in time of need.
Hebrews 4:16

If any of you lacks wisdom, let him ask God, who gives generously to all without reproach, and it will be given him. But let him ask in faith, with no doubting, for the one who doubts is like a wave of the sea that is driven and tossed by the wind. For that person must not suppose that he will receive anything from the Lord; he is a double-minded man, unstable in all his ways.
James 1:5–8

You do not have, because you do not ask.
James 4:2c

For whenever our heart condemns us, God is greater than our heart, and he knows everything. Beloved, if our heart does not condemn us, we have confidence before God; and whatever we ask we receive from him, because we keep his commandments and do what pleases him. And this is his commandment, that we believe in the name of his Son Jesus Christ and love one another, just as he has commanded us. Whoever keeps his commandments abides in God, and God in him. And by this we know that he abides in us, by the Spirit whom he has given us.
1 John 3:20–24

This is the confidence that we have toward him, that if we ask anything according to his will he hears us. And if we know that he hears us in what-

Be encouraged, dear Christian reader, with fresh earnestness to give yourself to prayer, if you can only be sure that you ask for things which are for the glory of God.

GEORGE MUELLER

Men may spurn our appeals, reject our message, oppose our arguments, despise our persons, but they are helpless against our prayers.

J. SIDLOW BAXTER

ever we ask, we know that we have the requests that we have asked of him.

1 John 5:14–15

If anyone sees his brother committing a sin not leading to death, he shall ask, and God will give him life—to those who commit sins that do not lead to death.

1 John 5:16a

Can any situation possibly arise in any circumstances, for which He is not adequate? Any pressure, promise, problem, responsibility or temptation of which Jesus Himself is not adequate?

W. IAN THOMAS

Prayer breaks all bars, dissolves all chains, opens all prisons, and widens all straits by which God's saints have been held.

E.M. BOUNDS

Additional Verses

Additional Verses

Additional Verses

PRAISE REPENT ASK **YIELD** EXPRESS THANKS REJOICE SHALOM.

Our God is in the heavens;
he does all that he pleases.

PSALM 115:3

Thou art all my good in times of peace,
my only support in days of trouble,
my one sufficiency when life shall end. . . .
Let me resign myself to thy wiser
determinations.

THE VALLEY OF VISION

YIELD

God Is Over All

ON EVERY SOJOURN, there are unexpected detours and challenging terrains. And, often, there is no way around them. The only way to proceed is to accept the difficult path, to press on; to yield. The biblical theme of yielding or surrendering is a powerful one. The Bible has far more to say about yielding than it does about asking.

Some examples:

Here, O Lord, hast thou placed us, and we will glorify thee here.

THOMAS C. UPHAM

- Noah built a ridiculously huge boat with no cargo and no body of water in sight, in obedience, Noah was yielding his will to God's: "[Noah] did all that God commanded him" (Genesis 6:22b).
- Abraham prepared to sacrifice his own son Isaac, with his own hands. "He cut the wood for the burnt offering and arose and went to the place of which God had told him" (Genesis 22:3b).
- Daniel turned away from the luxuries of a foreign culture and "resolved that he would not defile himself" (Daniel 1:8).
- Mary, the mother of Jesus, readily accepted the mysterious prediction of the angel, responding, "Behold, I am the servant of the Lord; let it be to me according to your word" (Luke 1:38).
- The writer of Hebrews encouraged early Christians saying, "You joyfully accepted the plundering of your property, since you knew that

you yourselves had a better possession and an abiding one" (Hebrews 10:34).

- Jesus' humble request of: "My Father, if it be possible, let this cup pass from me;" was punctuated with: "nevertheless, not as I will, but as you will" (Matthew 26:39; see also Mark 14:36 and Luke 22:42).

These people knew the truth of Psalm 31:14–15a: "I trust in you, O LORD; I say, 'You are my God.' My times are in your hand." Their trust in God's goodness to them allowed them to accept what they wouldn't have chosen for themselves.

Sometimes, yielding comes in the form of *waiting*; waiting while it appears as though God has forgotten all about me.

Andrew Murray expressed yielding in this way:

First, He brought me here, it is by His will I am in this [difficult] place: in that fact I will rest.

Next, He will keep me here in His love, and give me grace to behave as His child.

Then, He will make the trial a blessing, teaching me the lessons He intends me to learn, and working in me the grace He means to bestow.

Last, in His good time He can bring me out again—how and when He knows.

Let me say I am here,
(1) By God's appointment,
(2) In His keeping,
(3) Under His training
(4) For His time.

The strength of patience hangs on our capacity to believe that God is up to something good for us in all our delays and detours.

JOHN PIPER

We must remind ourselves to "Wait for the LORD; be strong, and let your heart take courage; wait for the LORD!" (Psalm 27:14) and that "the Lord will not cast off forever, but, though he cause grief, he will have compassion according to the abundance of his steadfast love; for he does not afflict from his heart or grieve the children of men" (Lamentations 3:31–33).

Sometimes, yielding comes in the form of *accepting*; accepting a hard providence. Paul submitted to his thorn in the flesh, proclaiming: "I will boast all the more gladly of my weaknesses, so that the power of Christ may rest upon me" (2 Corinthians 12:9b).

We *all* have crosses to bear *every day!* Jesus bluntly said it: "If anyone would come after me, let him deny himself and take up his cross daily and follow me" (Luke 9:23).

The psalmist models how we must preach truth to our weak hearts:

Some of His greatest mercies are His refusals. He says no in order that He may, in some way we cannot imagine, say yes. All His ways with us are merciful. His meaning is always love.

ELISABETH ELLIOT

- "My flesh and my heart may fail, but God is the strength of my heart and my portion forever." (Psalm 73:26)
- "It is good for me that I was afflicted, that I might learn your statutes." (Psalm 119:71)

With surrender, we get more of God. C. S. Lewis describes it like so:

> Christ says, "Give me All. I don't want so much of your time and so much of your money and so much of your work: I want you. . . . No half-measures are any good. . . . Hand over the whole . . . self, all the desires which you think innocent as well as the ones you think wicked—the whole outfit. I will give you a new self instead. I will give you Myself: my own will shall become yours."

What might seem like a very passive action—yielding—is necessary for our true refinement. The prophet Zechariah knew this when he put God's works into words: "I will . . . refine them as one refines silver, and test them as gold is tested. They will call upon my name, and I will answer them. I will say, 'They are my people'; and they will say, 'The LORD is my God'" (Zechariah 13:9).

To yield is to say: *"Yes!"* to God: "Yes" to what I want, "Yes" (or at least "I am willing . . .") to what I don't want. In so doing, I am submitting to His greater wisdom for my life. As Jesus subjected His will to His Father, so must we. "Not my will, but yours, be done" (Luke 22:42b). "He must increase, but I must decrease" (John 3:30).

God knows what a battle this is for us. Jesus struggled to yield His will to the Father's. He was with Jesus as He struggled to yield His will to the Father's. He saw His Son weep with His face on the ground of the world that they had created together. That struggle—that inward battle—is *not* sin. It is part of surrendering. But the more quickly we yield, the less painful the struggle. Becoming hardened, refusing to yield, saying, "No!" to God, *is* sin. Jesus warns: "Whoever does not take his cross and follow me is not worthy of me. Whoever finds his life will lose it, and whoever loses his life for my sake will find it" (Matthew 10:38–39). But He comforts us with the promise: "I give them eternal life, and they will never perish, and no one will snatch them out of my hand" (John 10:28). In yielding, we are safe.

Difficulties afford a platform upon which He can show Himself. Without them we could never know how tender, faithful, and Almighty our God is.

HUDSON TAYLOR

This balance of waiting and accepting while still expecting is not a mind game—it's a faith walk. I've been strengthened over and over by Psalm 69:

> As for me, my prayer is to you, O LORD.
>   At an acceptable time, O God,
>   in the abundance of your steadfast love answer me in your saving faithfulness. (v. 13)

> Answer me, O LORD, for your steadfast love is good;
>   according to your abundant mercy, turn to me. (v. 16)

If your schedule requires or if your heart feels ready to end your prayer time, *Yield* is a good place to stop. Being yielded is also a great position in which to continue on to *Express Thanks, Rejoice,* and *Shalom.* I know I am yielded to God when I can say: "Your will *is* my will."

PATH MARKER
Consider writing out your own lamentations. Yielding can be very hard. It is faith-building to look back and remember the ways God has worked in dark places.

A Prayer of Yielding

Dear Sovereign Father, Shepherd Lord, and Comforting Holy Spirit:

Help me to be so yielded to You that I steadily release my frail human will to Your powerful divine will. May I have eyes to see You as being *for* me even when it feels as if You're against me. May Your past faithfulnesses inspire me to trust You in the darkness of the night, in the uncertainty of the way. Help me to wait for *the acceptable time* of Your answer.

I am Yours.

Amen.

> *"But as for me, my prayer is to you, O Lord. At an acceptable time, O God, in the abundance of your steadfast love answer me in your saving faithfulness."*
> *Psalm 69:13*

PRAYER PASSAGES

And I will walk among you and will be your God, and you shall be my people.
Leviticus 26:12

The eternal God is your dwelling place, and underneath are the everlasting arms.
Deuteronomy 33:27a

And he said, "Naked I came from my mother's womb, and naked shall I return. The LORD gave, and the LORD has taken away; blessed be the name of the LORD."
Job 1:21

Agree with God, and be at peace; thereby good will come to you. Receive instruction from his mouth, and lay up his words in your heart.
Job 22:21–22

But he knows the way that I take; when he has tried me, I shall come out as gold.
Job 23:10

I will give thanks to the LORD with my whole heart; I will recount all of your wonderful deeds. I will be glad and exult in you; I will sing praise to your name, O Most High.
Psalm 9:1–2

Make me to know your ways, O LORD; teach me your paths. Lead me in your truth and teach me, for you are the God of my salvation; for you I wait all the day long.
Psalm 25:4–5

Trust the past to the mercy of God, the present to his love, and the future to his Providence.

ANONYMOUS

Enjoy the blessings of this day, if God sends them; and the evils of it bear patiently and sweetly; for this day is only ours, we are dead to yesterday, and we are not yet born to the morrow.

JEREMY TAYLOR

You have said, "Seek my face." My heart says to
you, "Your face, LORD, do I seek."
Psalm 27:8

I believe that I shall look upon the goodness of
the LORD in the land of the living! Wait for the
LORD; be strong, and let your heart take courage;
wait for the LORD!
Psalm 27:13–14

Blessed be the LORD! For he has heard the voice
of my pleas for mercy.
Psalm 28:6

For his anger is but for a moment, and his favor
is for a lifetime. Weeping may tarry for the night,
but joy comes with the morning.
Psalm 30:5

But I trust in you, O LORD; I say, "You are my
God." My times are in your hand.
Psalm 31:14–15a

I will instruct you and teach you in the way
you should go; I will counsel you with my eye
upon you.
Psalm 32:8

Delight yourself in the LORD, and he will give you
the desires of your heart. Commit your way to the
LORD; trust in him, and he will act.
Psalm 37:4–5

Be still before the LORD and wait patiently for him.
Psalm 37:7a

*We are walking through
this world under the eye
of our Heavenly Father.*
DAVID MARTYN
LLOYD-JONES

*Not one single prayer
of faith can possibly
be lost . . . persevering
prayer is irresistible,
prayer becomes the quiet,
persistent living of our life
of desire and faith in the
presence of our God.*
ANDREW MURRAY

O Lord, all my longing is before you; my sighing is not hidden from you. . . . But for you, O Lord, do I wait; it is you, O Lord my God, who will answer.
Psalm 38:9, 15

I waited patiently for the Lord; he inclined to me and heard my cry . . . making my steps secure.
Psalm 40:1–2

I delight to do your will, O my God; your law is within my heart.
Psalm 40:8

Be still, and know that I am God. I will be exalted among the nations, I will be exalted in the earth!
Psalm 46:10

This is God, our God forever and ever. He will guide us forever.
Psalm 48:14

As for me, my prayer is to you, O Lord. At an acceptable time, O God, in the abundance of your steadfast love answer me in your saving faithfulness. Answer me, O Lord, for your steadfast love is good; according to your abundant mercy, turn to me.
Psalm 69:13, 16

O God, from my youth you have taught me, and I still proclaim your wondrous deeds. So even to old age and gray hairs, O God, do not forsake me, until I proclaim your might to another generation, your power to all those to come. Your righteousness, O God, reaches the high heavens. You who have done great things, O God, who is like you?
Psalm 71:17–19

Thy way, not mine,
O Lord,
However dark it be!
Lead me by thine own
hand,
Choose out the path for
me.

Not mine, not mine the
choice,
In things or great or
small;
Be thou my guide, my
strength,
My wisdom, and my all.

HORATIUS BONAR

Nevertheless, I am continually with you; you hold my right hand. You guide me with your counsel, and afterward you will receive me to glory. Whom have I in heaven but you? And there is nothing on earth that I desire besides you. My flesh and my heart may fail, but God is the strength of my heart and my portion forever.

Psalm 73:23–26

For a day in your courts is better than a thousand elsewhere. I would rather be a doorkeeper in the house of my God than dwell in the tents of wickedness. For the LORD God is a sun and shield; the LORD bestows favor and honor. No good thing does he withhold from those who walk uprightly. O LORD of hosts, blessed is the one who trusts in you!

Psalm 84:10–12

Teach me your way, O LORD, that I may walk in your truth; unite my heart to fear your name.

Psalm 86:11

Let the favor of the Lord our God be upon us, and establish the work of our hands upon us; yes, establish the work of our hands!

Psalm 90:17

When the cares of my heart are many, your consolations cheer my soul.

Psalm 94:19

The LORD reigns! Yes, the world is established; it shall never be moved.

Psalm 96:10b

Trials are medicines which our gracious and wise physician gives because we need them, and he proportions the frequency and weight of them to what the care requires. Let us trust his skill and thank him for his prescription.

ISAAC NEWTON

Doubt everything, but believe in Christ.

ELIZABETH PRENTISS

Thy will be done. I yield up everything.

GEORGE MACDONALD

But the steadfast love of the LORD is from everlasting to everlasting on those who fear him, and his righteousness to children's children, to those who keep his covenant and remember to do his commandments. The LORD has established his throne in the heavens, and his kingdom rules over all.
Psalm 103:17–19

Our God is in the heavens; he does all that he pleases.
Psalm 115:3

O LORD, I am your servant.
Psalm 116:16a

Out of my distress I called on the LORD; the LORD answered me and set me free. The LORD is on my side; I will not fear. What can man do to me? The LORD is on my side as my helper.
Psalm 118:5–7a

I was pushed hard, so that I was falling, but the LORD helped me. The LORD is my strength and my song; he has become my salvation.
Psalm 118:13–14

Oh that my ways may be steadfast in keeping your statutes!
Psalm 119:5

It is good for me that I was afflicted, that I might learn your statutes.
Psalm 119:71

Forever, O LORD, your word is firmly fixed in the heavens. Your faithfulness endures to all genera-

Whatever the particular call is, the particular sacrifice God asks you to make, the particular cross He wishes you to embrace, whatever the particular path He wants you to tread, will you rise up, and say in your heart, "Yes, Lord, I accept it; I submit, I yield, I pledge myself to walk in that path, and to follow that Voice, and to trust Thee with the consequences"? Oh! but you say, "I don't know what He will want next." No, we none of us know that, but we know we shall be safe in His hands.

CATHERINE BOOTH

tions; you have established the earth, and it stands fast. By your appointment they stand this day, for all things are your servants.

Psalm 119:89–91

I incline my heart to perform your statutes forever, to the end.

Psalm 119:112

I lift up my eyes to the hills. From where does my help come? My help comes from the LORD, who made heaven and earth. He will not let your foot be moved; he who keeps you will not slumber. Behold, he who keeps Israel will neither slumber nor sleep. The LORD is your keeper; the LORD is your shade on your right hand. The sun shall not strike you by day, nor the moon by night. The LORD will keep you from all evil; he will keep your life. The LORD will keep your going out and your coming in from this time forth and forevermore.

Psalm 121

Unless the LORD builds the house, those who build it labor in vain. Unless the LORD watches over the city, the watchman stays awake in vain. It is in vain that you rise up early and go late to rest, eating the bread of anxious toil; for he gives to his beloved sleep.

Psalm 127:1–2

For I know that the LORD is great, and that our Lord is above all gods. Whatever the LORD pleases, he does, in heaven and on earth, in the seas and all deeps.

Psalm 135:5–6

God does not give us overcoming life; He gives life as we overcome. The strain is the strength. If there is no strain there is no strength. . . . Immediately you face the strain, you will get the strength.

OSWALD CHAMBERS

What God says is best, is best, though all the men in the world are against it.

JOHN BUNYAN

The LORD will fulfill his purpose for me; your steadfast love, O LORD, endures forever. Do not forsake the work of your hands.
Psalm 138:8

Teach me to do your will, for you are my God! Let your good Spirit lead me on level ground!
Psalm 143:10

In the path of righteousness is life, and in its pathway there is no death.
Proverbs 12:28

The LORD has made everything for its purpose, even the wicked for the day of trouble.
Proverbs 16:4

The lot is cast into the lap, but its every decision is from the LORD.
Proverbs 16:33

For everything there is a season, and a time for every matter under heaven: a time to be born, and a time to die; a time to plant, and a time to pluck up what is planted; a time to kill, and a time to heal; a time to break down, and a time to build up; a time to weep, and a time to laugh; a time to mourn, and a time to dance; a time to cast away stones, and a time to gather stones together; a time to embrace, and a time to refrain from embracing; a time to seek, and a time to lose; a time to keep, and a time to cast away; a time to tear, and a time to sew; a time to keep silence, and a time to speak; a time to love, and a time to hate; a time for war, and a time for peace.
Ecclesiastes 3:1–8

Let us sometimes in our prayers, when we are in danger of being preoccupied with our fervent, urgent petitions, as to forget that the Father knows and hears, let us hold still and just quietly say: My Father sees, My Father hears, My Father knows.

ANDREW MURRAY

The end of the matter; all has been heard. Fear God and keep his commandments, for this is the whole duty of man.

Ecclesiastes 12:13

And I heard the voice of the Lord saying, "Whom shall I send, and who will go for us?" Then I said, "Here I am! Send me."

Isaiah 6:8

Therefore the LORD waits to be gracious to you, and therefore he exalts himself to show mercy to you. For the LORD is a God of justice; blessed are all those who wait for him.

Isaiah 30:18

Can a woman forget her nursing child, that she should have no compassion on the son of her womb? Even these may forget, yet I will not forget you. Behold, I have engraved you on the palms of my hands.

Isaiah 49:15–16a

And the LORD will guide you continually and satisfy your desire in scorched places.

Isaiah 58:11a

Thus says the LORD: "Stand by the roads, and look, and ask for the ancient paths, where the good way is; and walk in it, and find rest for your souls."

Jeremiah 6:16a

But this command I gave them: "Obey my voice, and I will be your God, and you shall be my people. And walk in all the way that I command you, that it may be well with you."

Jeremiah 7:23

O LORD, who art our Guide even unto death, grant us, I pray Thee, grace to follow Thee whithersoever Thou goest. In little daily duties to which Thou callest us, bow down our wills to simple obedience, patience under pain or provocation, strict truthfulness of word and manner, humility, kindness; in great acts of duty or perfection, if Thou shouldest call us to them, uplift us to self-sacrifice, heroic courage, laying down life for Thy truth's sake, or for a brother. Amen.

CHRISTINA ROSSETTI

And they shall be my people, and I will be their God. I will give them one heart and one way, that they may fear me forever, for their own good and the good of their children after them. I will make with them an everlasting covenant, that I will not turn away from doing good to them. And I will put the fear of me in their hearts, that they may not turn from me. I will rejoice in doing them good, and I will plant them in this land in faithfulness, with all my heart and all my soul.
Jeremiah 32:38–41

But this I call to mind, and therefore I have hope: The steadfast love of the LORD never ceases; his mercies never come to an end; they are new every morning; great is your faithfulness. "The LORD is my portion," says my soul, "therefore I will hope in him." The LORD is good to those who wait for him, to the soul who seeks him. It is good that one should wait quietly for the salvation of the LORD.
Lamentations 3:21–26

For the Lord will not cast off forever, but, though he cause grief, he will have compassion according to the abundance of his steadfast love; for he does not afflict from his heart or grieve the children of men.
Lamentations 3:31–33

And I will give them one heart, and a new spirit I will put within them. I will remove the heart of stone from their flesh and give them a heart of flesh, that they may walk in my statutes and keep my rules and obey them. And they shall be my people, and I will be their God.
Ezekiel 11:19–20

None but God can satisfy the longings of an immortal soul; that as the heart was made for Him, so He only can fill it.

RICHARD CHENEVIX TRENCH

If we cannot work out the will of God where God has placed us, then why has He placed us there?

J. H. THOM

And I will give you a new heart, and a new spirit I
will put within you. And I will remove the heart
of stone from your flesh and give you a heart of
flesh. And I will put my Spirit within you, and
cause you to walk in my statutes and be careful to
obey my rules.
Ezekiel 36:26–27

My dwelling place shall be with them, and I will
be their God, and they shall be my people.
Ezekiel 37:27

Though the fig tree should not blossom, nor fruit
be on the vines, the produce of the olive fail and the
fields yield no food, the flock be cut off from the fold
and there be no herd in the stalls, yet I will rejoice in
the LORD; I will take joy in the God of my salvation.
GOD, the Lord, is my strength; he makes my feet
like the deer's; he makes me tread on my high places.
Habakkuk 3:17–19a

[I will] refine them as one refines silver, and test
them as gold is tested. They will call upon my name,
and I will answer them. I will say, "They are my
people"; and they will say, "The LORD is my God."
Zechariah 13:9b

Enter by the narrow gate. For the gate is wide and
the way is easy that leads to destruction, and those
who enter by it are many. For the gate is narrow
and the way is hard that leads to life, and those
who find it are few.
Matthew 7:13–14

Fear not, therefore; you are of more value than
many sparrows.
Matthew 10:31

*Never be afraid to trust
an unknown future to a
known God.*
CORRIE TEN BOOM

*Christ does not want to
be our helper; He wants
to be our life. He does not
want us to work for Him.
He wants us to let Him
do His work through
us, using us as we use a
pencil to write with.*
CHARLES G.
TRUMBULL

And whoever does not take his cross and follow me is not worthy of me. Whoever finds his life will lose it, and whoever loses his life for my sake will find it.
Matthew 10:38–39

Come to me, all who labor and are heavy laden, and I will give you rest. Take my yoke upon you, and learn from me, for I am gentle and lowly in heart, and you will find rest for your souls. For my yoke is easy, and my burden is light.
Matthew 11:28–30

Then Jesus told his disciples, "If anyone would come after me, let him deny himself and take up his cross and follow me. For whoever would save his life will lose it, but whoever loses his life for my sake will find it. For what will it profit a man if he gains the whole world and forfeits his soul? Or what shall a man give in return for his soul?"
Matthew 16:24–26

And calling to him a child, he put him in the midst of them and said, "Truly, I say to you, unless you turn and become like children, you will never enter the kingdom of heaven. Whoever humbles himself like this child is the greatest in the kingdom of heaven."
Matthew 18:2–4

Watch therefore, for you know neither the day nor the hour.
Matthew 25:13

And Mary said, "My soul magnifies the Lord, and my spirit rejoices in God my Savior, for he has

Conversion is not the smooth, easy-going process some men seem to think. . . . It is wounding work, this breaking of the hearts, but without wounding there is no saving. . . . Where there is grafting there will always be a cutting, the graft must be let in with a wound; to stick it onto the outside or to tie it on with a string would be of no use. Heart must be set to heart and back to back or there will be no sap from root to branch. And this, I say, must be done by a wound, by a cut.

JOHN BUNYAN

looked on the humble estate of his servant . . . for
he who is mighty has done great things for me,
and holy is his name."
Luke 1:46–48a, 49

And he said to all, "If anyone would come after
me, let him deny himself and take up his cross
daily and follow me. For whoever would save his
life will lose it, but whoever loses his life for my
sake will save it."
Luke 9:23–24

And [Jesus] . . . knelt down and prayed, saying,
"Father, if you are willing, remove this cup from
me. Nevertheless, not my will, but yours, be done."
Luke 22:41–42

He must increase, but I must decrease.
John 3:30

I give them eternal life, and they will never perish,
and no one will snatch them out of my hand. My
Father, who has given them to me, is greater than
all, and no one is able to snatch them out of the
Father's hand. I and the Father are one.
John 10:28–30

Let not your hearts be troubled. Believe in God;
believe also in me. . . . I will not leave you as
orphans; I will come to you.
John 14:1, 18

In the world you will have tribulation. But take
heart; I have overcome the world.
John 16:33b

*Take your burdens, and
troubles, and losses, and
wrongs, if come they
must and will, as your
opportunities, knowing
that God has girded you
for greater things than
these. Oh, to live out such
a life as God appoints,
how great a thing it is!*
HORACE BUSHNELL

Therefore, since we have been justified by faith, we have peace with God through our Lord Jesus Christ. Through him we have also obtained access by faith into this grace in which we stand, and we rejoice in hope of the glory of God. Not only that, but we rejoice in our sufferings, knowing that suffering produces endurance, and endurance produces character, and character produces hope, and hope does not put us to shame, because God's love has been poured into our hearts through the Holy Spirit who has been given to us.
Romans 5:1–5

When once our hearts are yielded to His service, God is working in us and through us. Hitherto, perhaps, our little world has only been large enough to hold self and the present. But, gradually, through tender leadings and unfoldings, and, it may be, through pain and suffering, we come to learn life's lesson, —that it is God's world, not ours.

HETTY BOWMAN

We know that for those who love God all things work together for good, for those who are called according to his purpose. . . . For I am sure that neither death nor life, nor angels nor rulers, nor things present nor things to come, nor powers, nor height nor depth, nor anything else in all creation, will be able to separate us from the love of God in Christ Jesus our Lord.
Romans 8:28, 38–39

Oh, the depth of the riches and wisdom and knowledge of God! How unsearchable are his judgments and how inscrutable his ways! "For who has known the mind of the Lord, or who has been his counselor?" "Or who has given a gift to him that he might be repaid?" For from him and through him and to him are all things. To him be glory forever. Amen.
Romans 11:33–36

God never gives strength for tomorrow or for the next hour, but only for the strain of the minute.

OSWALD CHAMBERS

Rejoice in hope, be patient in tribulation, be constant in prayer.
Romans 12:12

For it is written, "As I live, says the Lord, every knee shall bow to me, and every tongue shall confess to God." So then each of us will give an account of himself to God.

Romans 14:11–12

For Christ did not please himself, but as it is written, "The reproaches of those who reproached you fell on me." For whatever was written in former days was written for our instruction, that through endurance and through the encouragement of the Scriptures we might have hope.

Romans 15:3–4

So, whether you eat or drink, or whatever you do, do all to the glory of God.

1 Corinthians 10:31

God said, "I will make my dwelling among them and walk among them, and I will be their God, and they shall be my people."

2 Corinthians 6:16b

We only know ourselves and what we really are, when the force of circumstances bring us out.

ELIZABETH PRENTISS

"My grace is sufficient for you, for my power is made perfect in weakness." Therefore I will boast all the more gladly of my weaknesses, so that the power of Christ may rest upon me. For the sake of Christ, then, I am content with weaknesses, insults, hardships, persecutions, and calamities. For when I am weak, then I am strong.

2 Corinthians 12:9–10

God may not give us an easy journey to the Promised Land, but He will give us a safe one.

ANDREW BONAR

For through the law I died to the law, so that I might live to God. I have been crucified with Christ. It is no longer I who live, but Christ who lives in me. And the life I now live in the flesh I live by faith in the Son of God, who loved me and gave himself for me.

Galatians 2:19–20

Lord, be pleased to help and strengthen me in all this . . . in all my perplexities make a way where I see no way.

ELIZABETH FRY

Let me learn by paradox
that the way down is
the way up,
that to be low is to be
high,
that the broken heart is
the healed heart,
that the contrite spirit
is the rejoicing spirit,
that the repenting soul
is the victorious soul,
that to have nothing is
to possess all,
that to bear the cross is
to wear the crown,
that to give is to receive,
that the valley is the
place of vision. . . .
Let me find thy light in
my darkness,
thy life in my death,
thy joy in my sorrow,
thy grace in my sin,
thy riches in my
poverty,
thy glory in my valley.
THE VALLEY OF
VISION

For we are his workmanship, created in Christ Jesus for good works, which God prepared beforehand, that we should walk in them.
Ephesians 2:10

The Lord is at hand; do not be anxious about anything, but in everything by prayer and supplication with thanksgiving let your requests be made known to God. And the peace of God, which surpasses all understanding, will guard your hearts and your minds in Christ Jesus.
Philippians 4:5b–7

For you have died, and your life is hidden with Christ in God. When Christ who is your life appears, then you also will appear with him in glory.
Colossians 3:3–4

Whatever you do, work heartily, as for the Lord and not for men, knowing that from the Lord you will receive the inheritance as your reward. You are serving the Lord Christ.
Colossians 3:23–24

But as for you, O man of God, flee these things. Pursue righteousness, godliness, faith, love, steadfastness, gentleness. Fight the good fight of the faith. Take hold of the eternal life to which you were called and about which you made the good confession in the presence of many witnesses.
1 Timothy 6:11–12

But I am not ashamed, for I know whom I have believed, and I am convinced that he is able to guard until that Day what has been entrusted to me.
2 Timothy 1:12b

Count it all joy, my brothers, when you meet trials of various kinds, for you know that the testing of your faith produces steadfastness. And let steadfastness have its full effect, that you may be perfect and complete, lacking in nothing.
James 1:2–4

But be doers of the word, and not hearers only, deceiving yourselves.
James 1:22

In this you rejoice, though now for a little while, if necessary, you have been grieved by various trials, so that the tested genuineness of your faith—more precious than gold that perishes though it is tested by fire—may be found to result in praise and glory and honor at the revelation of Jesus Christ.
1 Peter 1:6–7

For to this you have been called, because Christ also suffered for you, leaving you an example, so that you might follow in his steps.
1 Peter 2:21

And after you have suffered a little while, the God of all grace, who has called you to his eternal glory in Christ, will himself restore, confirm, strengthen, and establish you. To him be the dominion forever and ever. Amen.
1 Peter 5:10–11

Do not love the world or the things in the world. If anyone loves the world, the love of the Father is not in him.
1 John 2:15

The light affliction is nothing, and the weight of glory is everything.

ELIZABETH PRENTISS

There are no "if's" in God's world. And no places that are safer than other places. The center of His will is our only safety . . . let's pray that we may always know it!

BETSIE TEN BOOM

....

....

....

....

....

....

By this we know that we abide in him and he in us, because he has given us of his Spirit.

1 John 4:13

Ye fearful saints, fresh
* courage take,*
The clouds ye so much
* dread*
Are big with mercy, and
* shall break*
In blessings on your head.
Judge not the Lord by
* feeble sense,*
But trust him for his
* grace;*
Behind a frowning
* providence*
He hides a smiling face.
His purposes will ripen
* fast,*
Unfolding ev'ry hour;
The bud may have a
* bitter taste,*
But sweet will be the flow'r.
Blind unbelief is sure to err
And scan his work in
* vain;*
God is his own
* interpreter,*
And He will make it
* plain.*

WILLIAM COWPER

Additional Verses

Additional Verses

PRAISE   REPENT   ASK   YIELD   **EXPRESS THANKS**   REJOICE   SHALOM.

I will give thanks to the LORD
with my whole heart;
I will recount all of your wonderful deeds.
I will be glad and exult in you;
I will sing praise to your name,
O Most High.

PSALM 9:1–2

Seek, as a plain duty,
to cultivate a buoyant, joyous sense
of the crowded kindnesses of God
in your daily life.

ALEXANDER MACLAREN

Express Thanks

God Is Giving

AFTER YIELDING TO GOD'S WILL FOR US, we thank Him. The Bible rings with words of gratitude. Christians are a grateful people.

- Mary's Magnificat: "For he who is mighty has done great things for me, and holy is his name" (Luke 1:49).
- The Gospels record that Jesus gave thanks to God before He fed the thousands (John 6:11), when He raised Lazarus from the dead (John 11:41), and when He served the Last Supper (Luke 22:17,19).
- The Epistles are full of examples of the apostles being thankful for their readers: "I thank my God in all my remembrance of you," (Philippians 1:3) and exhortations for their readers to be thankful: "And be thankful" (Colossians 3:15b).
- John's vision in Revelation: "We give thanks to you, Lord God Almighty, who is and who was" (Revelation 11:17a).

True Christians consider themselves not as satisfying some rigorous creditor, but as discharging a debt of gratitude.

WILLIAM WILBERFORCE

Paul, the often verbose apostle, gives this simple directive to an infant Church in a pagan territory beset with persecution:

Rejoice always, pray without ceasing, give thanks in all circumstances; for this is the will of God in Christ Jesus for you. (1 Thessalonians 5:16–18)

We often ponder what the will of God is in our lives, don't we? Here it is, in all of its demanding difficulty and in all of its sweet simplicity: Rejoice. Pray. Give thanks. Each instruction is underscored: *always*, *without ceasing*, in *all* circumstances.

In order to give thanks in *every* circumstance, I mustn't rely on my emotions. God determines the reality; my emotions don't always describe the truth. My emotions can lag behind and can even subvert truth. We can determine to be thankful in *any* situation, in *any* emotional condition. And an honest expression of thankfulness often stirs up our emotions to come along. It's okay to be sadly thankful. God is still honored in the honesty of determined gratitude.

Act for God, do and say the things that He will; direct your thoughts and intentions God-ward; and, depend upon it, in the slow process of nature, all that belongs to you—your instincts, your intelligence, your affections, your feelings— will gradually follow along the line of your action. Act for God; you are already showing love to Him and you will learn to feel it.

CHARLES GORE

Frances Ridley Havergal, authoress of many hymns (including "Take My Life and Let It Be" and "Like a River Glorious") and a frequent sufferer of emotional and physical pain, said: "We give thanks, often with a tearful doubtful voice."

Charles Haddon Spurgeon, in a sermon on Romans 1:20–21, gives some good insights into thankfulness. He says that people are prone to not thank God for what He's given, yet "The Lord continues to bless them in things temporal, to keep them in health and strength . . . and to give them the means of grace and spiritual opportunities; and they live as if these things were so commonplace that they were not worth thanking God for."

He compares us to the Israelites as they complained about the manna God gave them: "Thankless rebels! . . . We are few of us as thankful as we ought to be. . . . An unthankful spirit is, at bottom, an atheistic spirit. If God were God to us, we should not be unthankful to him. If God were glorified in our hearts, and we were thankful for everything that he did, we should walk in holiness, and live in submission."

Spurgeon closes this sermon with a charge—it's a very good template for a prayer of gratitude:

You that are saved must lead the song. "Bless the Lord, O my soul: and all that is within me, bless his holy name." Bless him for his Son. Bless him for his Spirit. Bless him for his Fatherhood. Bless him that you are his child. Bless him for what you have received. Bless him for what he has promised to give. Bless him for the past, the present, and the future. Bless him in every way, for everything, at all times, and in all places. Let all that is within you bless his holy name. Go your way rejoicing. May his Spirit help you so to do!

Thanking God is noticing Him by seeing what He has done. Expressing thanks focuses my fickle, oblivious heart; I'm led from yearning to contentment; from grasping for more to gasping in amazement. See what God has given!

PATH MARKER

Scan your life—the last 24 hours, the last week, the last decade or more—consider God's goodness to you. See it echoed across the ages in the verses in this section and give thanks. Consider starting a Thankfulness List to help you remember.

Prayer of Thanks

Dear Gracious Father, Bountiful Brother, and Gift-giving Holy Spirit:

We give thanks to You for You *are* good and you *do* good. You are generous and wise in all Your provisions.

We are grateful: grateful for what we know You've given us and done for us and grateful for the many things we don't see—the lifelong covenants, the daily graces, the moment-by-moment mercies, the confusing mysteries, the sweet provisions, and the painful providences. All are from Your strong hand and Your steadfast heart.

I am thankful.

Amen.

"I give thanks to you, O Lord my God, with my whole heart."
Psalm 86:11

PRAYER PASSAGES

Only fear the LORD and serve him faithfully with all your heart. For consider what great things he has done for you.
1 Samuel 12:24

Oh give thanks to the LORD; call upon his name; make known his deeds among the peoples! Sing to him, sing praises to him; tell of all his wondrous works! Glory in his holy name; let the hearts of those who seek the LORD rejoice! Seek the LORD and his strength; seek his presence continually! Remember the wondrous works that he has done, his miracles and the judgments he uttered.
1 Chronicles 16:8–12

Oh give thanks to the LORD, for he is good; for his steadfast love endures forever!
1 Chronicles 16:34

And now we thank you, our God, and praise your glorious name.
1 Chronicles 29:13

The LORD gave, and the LORD has taken away; blessed be the name of the LORD.
Job 1:21b

I will give to the LORD the thanks due to his righteousness, and I will sing praise to the name of the LORD, the Most High.
Psalm 7:17

When you glorify God as God, and are thankful for everything—when you can take up a bit of bread and a cup of cold water, and say with the poor Puritan, "What, all this, and Christ too?"—then are you happy, and you make others happy.

CHARLES HADDON
SPURGEON

I will give thanks to the LORD with my whole heart; I will recount all of your wonderful deeds. I will be glad and exult in you; I will sing praise to your name, O Most High.
Psalm 9:1–2

Surely goodness and mercy shall follow me all the days of my life, and I shall dwell in the house of the LORD forever.
Psalm 23:6

The LORD is my strength and my shield; in him my heart trusts, and I am helped; my heart exults, and with my song I give thanks to him.
Psalm 28:7

Sing praises to the LORD, O you his saints, and give thanks to his holy name. For his anger is but for a moment, and his favor is for a lifetime. Weeping may tarry for the night, but joy comes with the morning.
Psalm 30:4–5

O LORD my God, I will give thanks to you forever!
Psalm 30:12b

Oh, taste and see that the LORD is good! Blessed is the man who takes refuge in him!
Psalm 34:8

Offer to God a sacrifice of thanksgiving, and perform your vows to the Most High.
Psalm 50:14

Thou hast made me out of nothing,
hast recalled me from a far country,
hast translated me from ignorance to knowledge,
from darkness to light,
from death to life,
from misery to peace,
from folly to wisdom,
from error to truth,
from sin to victory.
Thanks be to thee for my high and holy calling.

THE VALLEY OF VISION

My heart is steadfast, O God, my heart is steadfast! I will sing and make melody! . . . I will give thanks to you, O Lord, among the peoples; I will sing praises to you among the nations. For your steadfast love is great to the heavens, your faithfulness to the clouds. Be exalted, O God, above the heavens! Let your glory be over all the earth!
Psalm 57:7, 9–11

Come and see what God has done: he is awesome in his deeds toward the children of man.
Psalm 66:5

I will praise the name of God with a song; I will magnify him with thanksgiving.
Psalm 69:30

My mouth will tell of your righteous acts, of your deeds of salvation all the day, for their number is past my knowledge.
Psalm 71:15

We give thanks to you, O God; we give thanks, for your name is near. We recount your wondrous deeds.
Psalm 75:1

I will remember the deeds of the LORD; yes, I will remember your wonders of old. I will ponder all your work, and meditate on your mighty deeds.
Psalm 77:11–12

But we your people, the sheep of your pasture, will give thanks to you forever; from generation to generation we will recount your praise.
Psalm 79:13

I would maintain that thanks are the highest form of thought, and that gratitude is happiness doubled by wonder.

G.K. CHESTERTON

Begin with thanking him for some little thing, and then go on, day by day, adding to your subjects of praise; thus you will find their numbers grow wonderfully: and in the same proportion, will your subjects of murmuring and complaining diminish, until you see in every thing some cause for thanksgiving.

PRISCILLA MAURICE

For a day in your courts is better than a thousand elsewhere. I would rather be a doorkeeper in the house of my God than dwell in the tents of wickedness. For the LORD God is a sun and shield; the LORD bestows favor and honor. No good thing does he withhold from those who walk uprightly.
Psalm 84:10–11

I give thanks to you, O Lord my God, with my whole heart, and I will glorify your name forever. For great is your steadfast love toward me.
Psalm 86:12–13a

It is good to give thanks to the LORD, to sing praises to your name, O Most High; to declare your steadfast love in the morning, and your faithfulness by night.
Psalm 92:1–2

Let us even at this present moment, though the skies be dark with clouds, yet give thanks unto his name.
CHARLES HADDON SPURGEON

Oh come, let us sing to the LORD; let us make a joyful noise to the rock of our salvation! Let us come into his presence with thanksgiving; let us make a joyful noise to him with songs of praise! For the LORD is a great God, and a great King above all gods.
Psalm 95:1–3

Upon thy bended knees, thank God for work. . . . For work to do, and strength to do the work, We thank Thee, Lord!
JOHN OXENHAM

For the LORD is good; his steadfast love endures forever, and his faithfulness to all generations.
Psalm 100:5

Thanksgiving stirreth up thankfulness in the heart.
JOHN PIPER

Oh give thanks to the LORD; call upon his name; make known his deeds among the peoples! Sing to him, sing praises to him; tell of all his wondrous works!
Psalms 105:1–2

Praise the LORD! Oh give thanks to the LORD, for he is good, for his steadfast love endures forever!
Psalm 106:1

Oh give thanks to the LORD, for he is good, for his steadfast love endures forever! . . . Let them thank the LORD for his steadfast love, for his wondrous works to the children of man!
Psalms 107:1, 15

Praise the LORD! I will give thanks to the LORD with my whole heart, in the company of the upright, in the congregation. Great are the works of the LORD, studied by all who delight in them. Full of splendor and majesty is his work, and his righteousness endures forever. He has caused his wondrous works to be remembered; the LORD is gracious and merciful. He provides food for those who fear him; he remembers his covenant forever.
Psalm 111:1–5

Oh give thanks to the LORD, for he is good; for his steadfast love endures forever! . . . You are my God, and I will give thanks to you; you are my God; I will extol you. Oh give thanks to the LORD, for he is good; for his steadfast love endures forever!
Psalm 118:1, 28–29

I thank you that you have answered me and have become my salvation.
Psalm 118:21

You are good and do good.
Psalm 119:68a

The unthankful heart . . . discovers no mercies; but let the thankful heart sweep through the day and, as the magnet finds the iron, so it will find, in every hour, some heavenly blessings!

HENRY WARD BEECHER

True thankfulness always glorifies God.

FRANS BAKKER

The LORD has done great things for us; we are glad.
Psalm 126:3

Give thanks to the LORD, for he is good, for his
steadfast love endures forever. Give thanks to the
God of gods, for his steadfast love endures forever.
Give thanks to the Lord of lords, for his steadfast
love endures forever; to him who alone does great
wonders, for his steadfast love endures forever;
to him who by understanding made the heavens,
for his steadfast love endures forever; to him who
spread out the earth above the waters, for his
steadfast love endures forever; to him who made
the great lights, for his steadfast love endures forever; the sun to rule over the day, for his steadfast
love endures forever; the moon and stars to rule
over the night, for his steadfast love endures forever. . . . Give thanks to the God of heaven, for his
steadfast love endures forever.
Psalm 136:1–9, 26

I give you thanks, O LORD, with my whole heart.
. . . On the day I called, you answered me; my
strength of soul you increased.
Psalm 138:1a, 3

One generation shall commend your works to
another, and shall declare your mighty acts. . . .
They shall speak of the might of your awesome
deeds, and I will declare your greatness.
Psalm 145:4–5

The LORD is good to all, and his mercy is over all
that he has made. All your works shall give thanks
to you, O LORD, and all your saints shall bless you!
Psalm 145:9–10

*Only he who gives thanks
for little things receives
the big things. . . . We
pray for the big things and
forget to give thanks for
the ordinary, small (and
yet really not small) gifts.
How can God entrust
great things to one who
will not thankfully receive
from Him the little things?*

DIETRICH
BONHOEFFER

154

Give thanks to the Lord, call upon his name, make known his deeds among the peoples, proclaim that his name is exalted.
Isaiah 12:4b

O Lord, you are my God; I will exalt you; I will praise your name, for you have done wonderful things, plans formed of old, faithful and sure.
Isaiah 25:1

I will recount the steadfast love of the Lord, the praises of the Lord, according to all that the Lord has granted us, and the great goodness to the house of Israel that he has granted them according to his compassion, according to the abundance of his steadfast love.
Isaiah 63:7

Give thanks to the Lord of hosts, for the Lord is good, for his steadfast love endures forever!
Jeremiah 33:11b

For he who is mighty has done great things for me, and holy is his name.
Luke 1:49

For from his fullness we have all received, grace upon grace.
John 1:16

For although they knew God, they did not honor him as God or give thanks to him, but they became futile in their thinking, and their foolish hearts were darkened.
Romans 1:21

Thou that has given so much to me give me one thing more, a grateful heart: not thankful when it pleaseth me, as if Thy blessings had spare days, but such a heart whose pulse may be Thy praise.

GEORGE HERBERT

Do you presume on the riches of his kindness and forbearance and patience, not knowing that God's kindness is meant to lead you to repentance?
Romans 2:4

I give thanks to my God always for you because of the grace of God that was given you in Christ Jesus.
1 Corinthians 1:4

Thanks be to God, who gives us the victory through our Lord Jesus Christ.
1 Corinthians 15:57

Thanks be to God, who in Christ always leads us in triumphal procession, and through us spreads the fragrance of the knowledge of him everywhere.
2 Corinthians 2:14

Thanks be to God for his inexpressible gift!
2 Corinthians 9:15

For this reason, because I have heard of your faith in the Lord Jesus and your love toward all the saints, I do not cease to give thanks for you, remembering you in my prayers, that the God of our Lord Jesus Christ, the Father of glory, may give you the Spirit of wisdom and of revelation in the knowledge of him, having the eyes of your hearts enlightened, that you may know what is the hope to which he has called you, what are the riches of his glorious inheritance in the saints, and what is the immeasurable greatness of his power toward us who believe, according to the working of his great might.
Ephesians 1:15–19

Seek, as a plain duty, to cultivate a buoyant, joyous sense of the crowded kindnesses of God in your daily life.

ALEXANDER
MACLAREN

Giving thanks always and for everything to God the Father in the name of our Lord Jesus Christ.
Ephesians 5:20

I thank my God in all my remembrance of you, always in every prayer of mine for you all making my prayer with joy.
Philippians 1:3–4

Do not be anxious about anything, but in everything by prayer and supplication with thanksgiving let your requests be made known to God.
Philippians 4:6

We always thank God, the Father of our Lord Jesus Christ, when we pray for you.
Colossians 1:3

And be thankful.
Colossians 3:15b

And whatever you do, in word or deed, do everything in the name of the Lord Jesus, giving thanks to God the Father through him.
Colossians 3:17

Continue steadfastly in prayer, being watchful in it with thanksgiving.
Colossians 4:2

We give thanks to God always for all of you, constantly mentioning you in our prayers.
1 Thessalonians 1:2

Let us thank God heartily as often as we pray that we have His Spirit in us to teach us to pray. Thanksgiving will draw our hearts out to God and keep us engaged with Him; it will take our attention from ourselves and give the Spirit room in our hearts.

ANDREW MURRAY

Now thank we all our God
with heart and hands
   and voices,
who wondrous things
   hath done,
in whom his world rejoices;
who from our mother's
   arms
hath blessed us on our way
with countless gifts of love,
and still is ours today.
O may this bounteous God
through all our life be
   near us,
with ever-joyful hearts
and blessed peace to cheer
   us;
and keep us in his grace,
and guide us when
   perplexed,
and free us from all ills
in this world and the next.

MARTIN RINKART

For what thanksgiving can we return to God for you, for all the joy that we feel for your sake before our God . . . ?
1 Thessalonians 3:9

Rejoice always, pray without ceasing, give thanks in all circumstances; for this is the will of God in Christ Jesus for you.
1 Thessalonians 5:16–18

First of all, then, I urge that supplications, prayers, intercessions, and thanksgivings be made for all people, for kings and all who are in high positions, that we may lead a peaceful and quiet life, godly and dignified in every way.
1 Timothy 2:1–2

For everything created by God is good, and nothing is to be rejected if it is received with thanksgiving, for it is made holy by the word of God and prayer.
1 Timothy 4:4

But understand this, that in the last days there will come times of difficulty. For people will be lovers of self, lovers of money, proud, arrogant, abusive, disobedient to their parents, ungrateful, unholy, heartless, unappeasable, slanderous, without self-control, brutal, not loving good, treacherous, reckless, swollen with conceit, lovers of pleasure rather than lovers of God, having the appearance of godliness, but denying its power. Avoid such people.
2 Timothy 3:2–5

But when the goodness and loving kindness of God our Savior appeared, he saved us, not because

of works done by us in righteousness, but according to his own mercy, by the washing of regeneration and renewal of the Holy Spirit, whom he poured out on us richly through Jesus Christ our Savior, so that being justified by his grace we might become heirs according to the hope of eternal life.
Titus 3:4–7

Therefore let us be grateful for receiving a kingdom that cannot be shaken, and thus let us offer to God acceptable worship, with reverence and awe.
Hebrews 12:28

Every good gift and every perfect gift is from above, coming down from the Father of lights with whom there is no variation or shadow due to change.
James 1:17

We give thanks to you, Lord God Almighty, who is and who was, for you have taken your great power and begun to reign.
Revelation 11:17

All praise and thanks to God
the Father now be given,
the Son, and Holy Ghost,
supreme in highest heaven,
the one eternal God,
whom earth and heaven adore;
for thus it was, is now,
and shall be evermore.

MARTIN RINKART

Additional Verses

Additional Verses

Additional Verses

Let the righteous one
rejoice in the LORD and
take refuge in him!

PSALM 64:10a

This is the happy life,
to rejoice to Thee,
of Thee, for Thee;
this it is, and there is no other.

AUGUSTINE OF HIPPO

REJOICE

God Sings Over Me

SOMETIMES, AS WE END A PRAYER TIME, our hearts leap and rejoicing comes easily. At other times, our hearts are heavy and joy is elusive. Neither experience is a judgment of the efficacy of our prayers. We can't make the joy happen. But we can choose to *rejoice* as we take *refuge* in Him.

Jesus' people have always lived with grief-tinged joy. Both sadness and joy are woven through the Epistles of the New Testament and into our lives today. Our Lord Jesus knew sadness: "He was . . . a man of sorrows, and acquainted with grief" (Isaiah 53:3a) yet He came to be our joy: "These things I have spoken to you, that my joy may be in you, and that your joy may be full" (John 15:11).

We've been told to "Rejoice with those who rejoice, weep with those who weep" (Romans 12:15). We are the "sorrowful, yet always rejoicing" people (2 Corinthians 6:10a).

As we live this life of tempered joy, we anticipate heaven where we will never sorrow again because "He will wipe away every tear from their eyes, and death shall be no more, neither shall there be mourning, nor crying, nor pain anymore, for the former things have passed away" (Revelation 21:4).

The only help for our sadness is to take *refuge* in God. This is actually an act of *rejoicing* in Him. It is

Our joy in Him may be a fluctuating thing: His joy in us knows no change.

HUDSON TAYLOR

showing Him—and my hurting heart—that He is all my security.

We must remember that God chooses to dwell with those who are low and contrite. The fact that He dwells with us may sometimes be our only reason for rejoicing on our weary way. "For thus says the One who is high and lifted up, who inhabits eternity, whose name is Holy: 'I dwell in the high and holy place, and also with him who is of a contrite and lowly spirit, to revive the spirit of the lowly, and to revive the heart of the contrite'" (Isaiah 57:15). He dwells with us to revive us. Amazing.

Prayer should be the means by which I, at all times, receive all that I need, and, for this reason, be my daily refuge, my daily consolation, my daily joy, my source of rich and inexhaustible joy in life.

OLE HALLESBY

All parents know the feeling of having a child flee to them in a moment of terror from a nightmare or a daytime scare. We know the child is saying, as he rushes into our arms: "You are what I need. Now!" In that exclusive place of protection is an intuitive sense of joy. The child is seeking safety but he also gets joy.

David, who was very familiar with being besieged, physically and emotionally, knew the need for taking refuge and the joy that is found there:

Let all who take refuge in you rejoice; let them ever sing for joy, and spread your protection over them, that those who love your name may exult in you. For you bless the righteous, O LORD; you cover him with favor as with a shield. (Psalm 5:11–12)

They tell what God has brought about and ponder what he has done. Let the righteous one rejoice in the LORD and take refuge in him! Let all the upright in heart exult! (Psalm 64:9b–10)

We must take refuge from God in God.

A. W. TOZER

Joy is central to Jesus' agenda for us. Heaven-grounded, not earthbound, joy. He said:

- "Rejoice that your names are written in heaven" (Luke 10:20b).
- "These things I have spoken to you, that my joy may be in you, and that your joy may be full" (John 15:11).

- "Your hearts will rejoice, and no one will take your joy from you" (John 16:22).

Joys are always on their way to us. They are always traveling to us through the darkness of the night. There is never a night when they are not coming.

AMY CARMICHAEL

Ponder this: God rejoiced over each of His redeemed at our conversion. "There will be more joy in heaven over one sinner who repents than over ninety-nine righteous persons who need no repentance" (Luke 15:7).

God rejoices over us still: "The LORD your God is in your midst, a mighty one who will save; he will rejoice over you with gladness; he will quiet you by his love; he will exult over you with loud singing" (Zephaniah 3:17).

As you journey in the varied joys and griefs of your life, fellow traveler, take refuge in the knowledge that God is rejoicing over you. His is a mighty joy. And it's more than a sweet emotion—it's secure dwelling place.

Preserve me, O God, for in you I take refuge.
I say to the LORD, "You are my Lord;
    I have no good apart from you." (Psalm 16:1)

You make known to me the path of life;
    in your presence there is fullness of joy;
    at your right hand are pleasures forevermore. (Psalm 16:11)

PATH MARKER

Don't try to manufacture joy. Settle into your sadness but seek God. Joy is where He is; it is what He is. Perhaps *rejoicing* will be kindled as you take *refuge* in Him.

A Prayer of Refuge and Rejoicing

Dear Eternal Rock, Storm-stilling Christ, and
Calming Holy Spirit:

You are our only refuge in the storms of life; our deepest joy in the tumult. To You I should run—my tower. Too often I retreat into my fears—the dark, dangerous dungeon of lies—instead of running to the strong, protective tower of Your love. Please rescue me from my consuming fears with Your anchoring hope and Your steadfast joy. *In You I live and move and have my being.* May my heart be strung in such a way as to pulse with Your tomb-rending joy. May Your song over me be louder than the fears within me. Under Your shadow, I *will* sing for joy.

I have You.

Amen.

"The Lord your God is in your midst, a mighty one who will save;
he will rejoice over you with gladness, he will quiet you by his love."
Zephaniah 3:17

PRAYER PASSAGES

He said, "The LORD is my rock and my fortress and my deliverer, my God, my rock, in whom I take refuge, my shield, and the horn of my salvation, my stronghold and my refuge, my savior. . . . I call upon the LORD, who is worthy to be praised."
2 Samuel 22:2–3a, 4a

This God—his way is perfect; the word of the LORD proves true; he is a shield for all those who take refuge in him. "For who is God, but the LORD? And who is a rock, except our God? This God is my strong refuge and has made my way blameless. He made my feet like the feet of a deer and set me secure on the heights. . . . You have given me the shield of your salvation, and your gentleness made me great."
2 Samuel 22:31–34, 36

Blessed be the LORD, the God of Israel, from everlasting to everlasting! Then all the people said, "Amen!" and praised the LORD.
1 Chronicles 16:36

The joy of the LORD is your strength.
Nehemiah 8:10b

But you, O LORD, are a shield about me, my glory, and the lifter of my head. I cried aloud to the LORD, and he answered me from his holy hill.
Psalm 3:3–4

But let all who take refuge in you rejoice; let them ever sing for joy, and spread your protection over

Joy is the serious business of Heaven.
C. S. LEWIS

*Remember, O my soul,
It is thy duty and
privilege
    to rejoice in God. . . .
He who is the ground of
    thy faith should be the
    substance of thy joy.*
THE VALLEY OF
VISION

them, that those who love your name may exult in you. For you bless the righteous, O LORD; you cover him with favor as with a shield.
Psalm 5:11–12

The LORD has heard my plea; the LORD accepts my prayer.
Psalm 6:9

The LORD is a stronghold for the oppressed, a stronghold in times of trouble. And those who know your name put their trust in you, for you, O LORD, have not forsaken those who seek you.
Psalm 9:9–10

I have trusted in your steadfast love; my heart shall rejoice in your salvation. I will sing to the LORD, because he has dealt bountifully with me.
Psalm 13:5–6

Preserve me, O God, for in you I take refuge. I say to the LORD, "You are my Lord; I have no good apart from you."
Psalm 16:1–2

The gracious soul dwells in God, is at home in him, and there dwells at ease, is in him perpetually pleased; and whatever he meets with in the world to make him uneasy, he finds enough in God to balance it.

MATTHEW HENRY

You make known to me the path of life; in your presence there is fullness of joy; at your right hand are pleasures forevermore.
Psalm 16:11

Wondrously show your steadfast love, O Savior of those who seek refuge from their adversaries at your right hand. Keep me as the apple of your eye; hide me in the shadow of your wings.
Psalm 17:7–8

The LORD is my rock and my fortress and my deliverer, my God, my rock, in whom I take refuge, my shield, and the horn of my salvation, my stronghold.
Psalm 18:2

This God—his way is perfect; the word of the LORD proves true; he is a shield for all those who take refuge in him. For who is God, but the LORD? And who is a rock, except our God?
Psalm 18:30–31

May the LORD answer you in the day of trouble! May the name of the God of Jacob protect you! May he send you help from the sanctuary and give you support from Zion! May he remember all your offerings and regard with favor your burnt sacrifices! *Selah* May he grant you your heart's desire and fulfill all your plans! May we shout for joy over your salvation, and in the name of our God set up our banners! May the LORD fulfill all your petitions! Now I know that the LORD saves his anointed; he will answer him from his holy heaven with the saving might of his right hand. Some trust in chariots and some in horses, but we trust in the name of the LORD our God. They collapse and fall, but we rise and stand upright. O LORD, save the king! May he answer us when we call.
Psalm 20

Oh, guard my soul, and deliver me! Let me not be put to shame, for I take refuge in you.
Psalm 25:20

The LORD is my light and my salvation; whom shall I fear? The LORD is the stronghold of my life; of whom shall I be afraid?
Psalm 27:1

In every gladness, Lord, Thou art The deeper Joy behind.

GEORGE
MACDONALD

One thing have I asked of the LORD, that will I seek after: that I may dwell in the house of the LORD all the days of my life, to gaze upon the beauty of the LORD and to inquire in his temple. For he will hide me in his shelter in the day of trouble; he will conceal me under the cover of his tent; he will lift me high upon a rock.

Psalm 27:4–5

Sing praises to the LORD, O you his saints, and give thanks to his holy name. For his anger is but for a moment, and his favor is for a lifetime. Weeping may tarry for the night, but joy comes with the morning.

Psalm 30:4–5

You have turned for me my mourning into dancing; you have loosed my sackcloth and clothed me with gladness, that my glory may sing your praise and not be silent. O LORD my God, I will give thanks to you forever!

Psalm 30:11–12

Christ for us is all our righteousness before a holy God; Christ in us is all our strength in an ungodly world.

ROBERT MURRAY M'CHEYNE

You are a hiding place for me; you preserve me from trouble; you surround me with shouts of deliverance. *Selah*

Psalm 32:7

Be glad in the LORD, and rejoice, O righteous, and shout for joy, all you upright in heart!

Psalm 32:11

God cannot give us a happiness and peace apart from Him because it is not there. There is no such thing.

C. S. LEWIS

The LORD is near to the brokenhearted and saves the crushed in spirit.

Psalm 34:18

Let those who delight in my righteousness shout for joy and be glad and say evermore, "Great is the LORD, who delights in the welfare of his servant!" Then my tongue shall tell of your righteousness and of your praise all the day long.

Psalm 35:27–28

God is our refuge and strength, a very present help in trouble.

Psalm 46:1

Clap your hands, all peoples! Shout to God with loud songs of joy! For the LORD, the Most High, is to be feared, a great king over all the earth. He subdued peoples under us, and nations under our feet. He chose our heritage for us, the pride of Jacob whom he loves. *Selah* God has gone up with a shout, the LORD with the sound of a trumpet. Sing praises to God, sing praises! Sing praises to our King, sing praises! For God is the King of all the earth; sing praises with a psalm! God reigns over the nations; God sits on his holy throne. The princes of the peoples gather as the people of the God of Abraham. For the shields of the earth belong to God; he is highly exalted!

Psalm 47

Restore to me the joy of your salvation, and uphold me with a willing spirit.

Psalm 51:12

Be merciful to me, O God, be merciful to me, for in you my soul takes refuge; in the shadow of your wings I will take refuge, till the storms of destruction pass by. I cry out to God Most High, to God who fulfills his purpose for me.

Psalm 57:1–2

*Joyful, joyful, we adore
Thee,
God of glory, Lord of love;
Hearts unfold like flow'rs
before Thee,
Op'ning to the sun above.
Melt the clouds of sin and
sadness;
Drive the dark of doubt
away;
Giver of immortal
gladness,
Fill us with the light of
day!*

HENRY J. VAN DYKE

O my Strength, I will watch for you, for you, O God, are my fortress.
Psalm 59:9

But I will sing of your strength; I will sing aloud of your steadfast love in the morning. For you have been to me a fortress and a refuge in the day of my distress. O my Strength, I will sing praises to you, for you, O God, are my fortress, the God who shows me steadfast love.
Psalm 59:16–17

Hear my cry, O God, listen to my prayer; from the end of the earth I call to you when my heart is faint. Lead me to the rock that is higher than I, for you have been my refuge, a strong tower against the enemy. Let me dwell in your tent forever! Let me take refuge under the shelter of your wings! *Selah*
Psalm 61:1–4

For God alone, O my soul, wait in silence, for my hope is from him. He only is my rock and my salvation, my fortress; I shall not be shaken. On God rests my salvation and my glory; my mighty rock, my refuge is God. Trust in him at all times, O people; pour out your heart before him; God is a refuge for us. *Selah*
Psalm 62:5–8

So I have looked upon you in the sanctuary, beholding your power and glory. Because your steadfast love is better than life, my lips will praise you. So I will bless you as long as I live; in your name I will lift up my hands. My soul will be satisfied as with fat and rich food, and my mouth will

The all-victorious Christ is like a great rock in a weary land, to whose shelter we may flee in every time of sorrow or trial, finding quiet refuge and peace in him.

J. R. MILLER

praise you with joyful lips, when I remember you
upon my bed, and meditate on you in the watches
of the night; for you have been my help, and in the
shadow of your wings I will sing for joy.
Psalm 63:2–7

They tell what God has brought about and ponder
what he has done. Let the righteous one rejoice
in the LORD and take refuge in him! Let all the
upright in heart exult!
Psalm 64:9b–10

But truly God has listened; he has attended to the
voice of my prayer. Blessed be God, because he has
not rejected my prayer or removed his steadfast
love from me!
Psalm 66:19–20

Let the nations be glad and sing for joy, for you
judge the peoples with equity and guide the
nations upon earth. *Selah* Let the peoples praise
you, O God; let all the peoples praise you!
Psalm 67:4–5

But the righteous shall be glad; they shall exult
before God; they shall be jubilant with joy! Sing
to God, sing praises to his name; lift up a song to
him who rides through the deserts; his name is the
LORD; exult before him!
Psalm 68:3–4

May all who seek you rejoice and be glad in you!
May those who love your salvation say evermore,
"God is great!"
Psalm 70:4

*The happiness of the
creature consists in
rejoicing in God, by
which also God is
magnified and exalted.*

JONATHAN
EDWARDS

My lips will shout for joy, when I sing praises to you; my soul also, which you have redeemed. And my tongue will talk of your righteous help all the day long.
Psalm 71:23–24a

May his name endure forever, his fame continue as long as the sun! May people be blessed in him, all nations call him blessed! Blessed be the LORD, the God of Israel, who alone does wondrous things. Blessed be his glorious name forever; may the whole earth be filled with his glory! Amen and Amen!
Psalm 72:17–19

But for me it is good to be near God; I have made the Lord GOD my refuge, that I may tell of all your works.
Psalm 73:28

Satisfy us in the morning with your steadfast love, that we may rejoice and be glad all our days.
Psalm 90:14

A mighty fortress is our
God, a bulwark never
*   failing;*
Our helper He, amid
the flood of mortal ills
*   prevailing:*
For still our ancient foe
doth seek to work us woe;
His craft and power are
great, and, armed with
*   cruel hate,*
On earth is not his equal.
MARTIN LUTHER

For you, O LORD, have made me glad by your work; at the works of your hands I sing for joy.
Psalm 92:4

The LORD reigns!
Psalm 96:10b

Rejoice in the LORD, O you righteous, and give thanks to his holy name!
Psalm 97:12

Bless the LORD, O you his angels, you mighty ones who do his word, obeying the voice of his

word! Bless the LORD, all his hosts, his ministers, who do his will! Bless the LORD, all his works, in all places of his dominion. Bless the LORD, O my soul!
Psalm 103:20–22

May the glory of the LORD endure forever; may the LORD rejoice in his works, who looks on the earth and it trembles, who touches the mountains and they smoke! I will sing to the LORD as long as I live; I will sing praise to my God while I have being. May my meditation be pleasing to him, for I rejoice in the LORD.
Psalm 104:31–34

Oh give thanks to the LORD; call upon his name; make known his deeds among the peoples! Sing to him, sing praises to him; tell of all his wondrous works! Glory in his holy name; let the hearts of those who seek the LORD rejoice! Seek the LORD and his strength; seek his presence continually! Remember the wondrous works that he has done.
Psalm 105:1–5a

Glory in his holy name; let the hearts of those who seek the LORD rejoice!
Psalm 105:3

Blessed be the LORD, the God of Israel, from everlasting to everlasting! And let all the people say, "Amen!" Praise the LORD!
Psalm 106:48

I was pushed hard, so that I was falling, but the LORD helped me. The LORD is my strength and my song; he has become my salvation.
Psalm 118:13–14

O Lord God,
Thou art my protecting
*   arm,*
fortress, refuge, shield,
*   buckler.*
Fight for me and my foes
*   must flee;*
Uphold me and I cannot
*   fall;*
Strengthen me and
*   I stand unmoved,*
*   unmoveable.*
THE VALLEY OF
VISION

The LORD has done great things for us; we are glad. . . . Those who sow in tears shall reap with shouts of joy! He who goes out weeping, bearing the seed for sowing, shall come home with shouts of joy, bringing his sheaves with him.
Psalm 126:3, 5–6

You hem me in, behind and before, and lay your hand upon me. Such knowledge is too wonderful for me; it is high; I cannot attain it. Where shall I go from your Spirit? Or where shall I flee from your presence? If I ascend to heaven, you are there! If I make my bed in Sheol, you are there! If I take the wings of the morning and dwell in the uttermost parts of the sea, even there your hand shall lead me, and your right hand shall hold me. If I say, "Surely the darkness shall cover me, and the light about me be night," even the darkness is not dark to you; the night is bright as the day, for darkness is as light with you.
Psalm 139:5–12

The name of the LORD is a strong tower; the righteous man runs into it and is safe.
Proverbs 18:10

It will be said on that day, "Behold, this is our God; we have waited for him, that he might save us. This is the LORD; we have waited for him; let us be glad and rejoice in his salvation."
Isaiah 25:9

The sun shall be no more your light by day, nor for brightness shall the moon give you light; but the LORD will be your everlasting light, and your God will be your glory. Your sun shall no more go down, nor your moon withdraw itself; for the

There is not one blade of grass, there is no color in this world that is not intended to make us rejoice.

JOHN CALVIN

LORD will be your everlasting light, and your days of mourning shall be ended.
Isaiah 60:19–20

I will greatly rejoice in the LORD; my soul shall exult in my God, for he has clothed me with the garments of salvation; he has covered me with the robe of righteousness, as a bridegroom decks himself like a priest with a beautiful headdress, and as a bride adorns herself with her jewels. For as the earth brings forth its sprouts, and as a garden causes what is sown in it to sprout up, so the Lord GOD will cause righteousness and praise to sprout up before all the nations.
Isaiah 61:10–11

I will turn their mourning into joy; I will comfort them, and give them gladness for sorrow.
Jeremiah 31:13b

The LORD is good, a stronghold in the day of trouble; he knows those who take refuge in him.
Nahum 1:7

Though the fig tree should not blossom, nor fruit be on the vines, the produce of the olive fail and the fields yield no food, the flock be cut off from the fold and there be no herd in the stalls, yet I will rejoice in the LORD; I will take joy in the God of my salvation.
Habakkuk 3:17–18

The LORD your God is in your midst, a mighty one who will save; he will rejoice over you with gladness; he will quiet you by his love; he will exult over you with loud singing.
Zephaniah 3:17

I have a longing for the
world above
where multitudes sing the
great song,
for my soul was never
created to love
the dust of the earth.

THE VALLEY OF
VISION

Simon Peter answered him, "Lord, to whom shall we go? You have the words of eternal life, and we have believed, and have come to know, that you are the Holy One of God."
John 6:68–69

Truly, truly, I say to you, you will weep and lament, but the world will rejoice. You will be sorrowful, but your sorrow will turn into joy. When a woman is giving birth, she has sorrow because her hour has come, but when she has delivered the baby, she no longer remembers the anguish, for joy that a human being has been born into the world. So also you have sorrow now, but I will see you again, and your hearts will rejoice, and no one will take your joy from you. In that day you will ask nothing of me. Truly, truly, I say to you, whatever you ask of the Father in my name, he will give it to you. Until now you have asked nothing in my name. Ask, and you will receive, that your joy may be full.
John 16:20–24

For David says concerning him, "I saw the Lord always before me, for he is at my right hand that I may not be shaken; therefore my heart was glad, and my tongue rejoiced; my flesh also will dwell in hope. . . . You have made known to me the paths of life; you will make me full of gladness with your presence."
Acts 2:25–26, 28

May the God of hope fill you with all joy and peace in believing, so that by the power of the Holy Spirit you may abound in hope.
Romans 15:13

Finally, brothers, rejoice.
2 Corinthians 13:11a

You are our light and our salvation, the stronghold and sanctuary in whom we find refuge. You refresh our souls daily with joys we cannot fathom nor fully count.

JOHN MACARTHUR

There is a joy which is not given to the ungodly, but to those who love Thee for Thine own sake, whose joy Thou Thyself art. And this is the happy life, to rejoice to Thee, of Thee, for Thee; this it is, and there is no other.

AUGUSTINE OF HIPPO

Rejoice in the Lord always; again I will say, rejoice.
Philippians 4:4

May you be strengthened with all power, according to his glorious might, for all endurance and patience with joy, giving thanks to the Father, who has qualified you to share in the inheritance of the saints in light. He has delivered us from the domain of darkness and transferred us to the kingdom of his beloved Son, in whom we have redemption, the forgiveness of sins.
Colossians 1:11–14

Rejoice always, pray without ceasing, give thanks in all circumstances; for this is the will of God in Christ Jesus for you.
1 Thessalonians 5:16–18

We who have fled for refuge might have strong encouragement to hold fast to the hope set before us. We have this as a sure and steadfast anchor of the soul, a hope that enters into the inner place behind the curtain, where Jesus has gone as a forerunner on our behalf, having become a high priest forever after the order of Melchizedek.
Hebrews 6:18b–20

Blessed be the God and Father of our Lord Jesus Christ! According to his great mercy, he has caused us to be born again to a living hope through the resurrection of Jesus Christ from the dead, to an inheritance that is imperishable, undefiled, and unfading, kept in heaven for you, who by God's power are being guarded through faith for a salvation ready to be revealed in the last time.
1 Peter 1:3–5

When the storm is loud, and the night is dark, and the soul is sad, and the heart oppressed . . . then, as weary travelers, may we look to Thee; and beholding the light of Thy love, may it bear us on, until we learn to sing Thy song in the night.

GEORGE DAWSON

If you are one of the King's pilgrims, you are quite safe.

HELEN L. TAYLOR

But rejoice insofar as you share Christ's sufferings, that you may also rejoice and be glad when his glory is revealed.

1 Peter 4:13

See what kind of love the Father has given to us, that we should be called children of God; and so we are. The reason why the world does not know us is that it did not know him. Beloved, we are God's children now, and what we will be has not yet appeared; but we know that when he appears we shall be like him, because we shall see him as he is.

1 John 3:1–2

Holy, holy, holy, is the Lord God Almighty, who was and is and is to come! . . . Worthy are you, our Lord and God, to receive glory and honor and power, for you created all things, and by your will they existed and were created.

Revelation 4:8b, 11

Amen! Blessing and glory and wisdom and thanksgiving and honor and power and might be to our God forever and ever! Amen.

Revelation 7:12

And from the throne came a voice saying, "Praise our God, all you his servants, you who fear him, small and great." Then I heard what seemed to be the voice of a great multitude, like the roar of many waters and like the sound of mighty peals of thunder, crying out, "Hallelujah! For the Lord our God the Almighty reigns."

Revelation 19:5–6

O Lord, Our Refuge from the storm, hide us, we entreat Thee, in Thine own Presence from the provoking of all men. By Thy holy love and fear, keep us from sins of temper and tongue.

CHRISTINA
ROSSETTI

He will wipe away every tear from their eyes, and death shall be no more, neither shall there be mourning, nor crying, nor pain anymore, for the former things have passed away.

Revelation 21:4

And now unto him who is able to keep us from falling and lift us from the dark valley of despair to the mountains of hope, from the midnight of desperation to the daybreak of joy; to him be power and authority, for ever and ever. Amen.

MARTIN LUTHER KING JR.

Additional Verses

Additional Verses

Additional Verses

[Jesus said:] Peace I leave with you;
my peace I give to you.
Not as the world gives do I give to you.
Let not your hearts be troubled,
neither let them be afraid.

JOHN 14:27

To him belong glory and dominion
forever and ever. Amen.

1 PETER 4:11c

Glory be to the Father;
And to the Son,
And to the Holy Ghost;
As it was in the beginning,
is now, and ever shall be,
World without end,
Amen, Amen.

GLORIA PATRI

SHALOM.

God Has Heard My Prayer

WE HAVE PRAISED, and repented, and asked, and yielded, and thanked, and rejoiced. Now we close our prayer time in peace. The last step of Prayer PathWay is *Shalom*.

This section of verses and quotes focus on the gentle but powerful themes of *selah* and *shalom*.

- *Selah* is a Hebrew word that's meaning is unclear—it's thought to suggest a musical interlude or *pause* to reflect upon what has gone before.
- *Shalom* is Hebrew for *peace*, but its meaning is more complex than just lack of conflict. It communicates "completeness and safety," a sense of well-being.[1] Even today it is sometimes used in farewell.

As we end our prayer time, we can pause to reflect or we can say "Amen" in peace. We often just slap "Amen" on at the end of our prayers, as if to say: "The End," but that is not what the word means. It is much more than a closing comment. *Amen* means "Let it be so."

Christ has said "Amen" to us. He is God's "Amen" to us. God says "Amen" to us through Christ in the cross, and we respond with "Amen" to God through Christ in . . . prayer.

JOHN PIPER

---

1. Walter A. Elwell, ed., *Evangelical Dictionary of Biblical Theology*, s.v. "Peace," (Grand Rapids: Baker Books, 1996), accessed Sept. 29, 2016, http://www.biblestudy tools.com/dictionary/peace/.

Revelation 3:14 uses "The Amen" as a name for Jesus; He is "the faithful and true witness." Jesus has been a witness of our prayer and He's been a witness to us. He has informed our praying because He has been interceding for us (Romans 8:34, Hebrews 7:25).

Through the day:
You keep him in perfect peace whose mind is stayed on you, because he trusts in you.

ISAIAH 26:3

When we say: "In Jesus' Name, Amen," we're echoing the powerful truth of 2 Corinthians 1:20–22: "For all the promises of God find their Yes in him. That is why it is through him that we utter our Amen to God for his glory. And it is God who establishes us with you in Christ, and has anointed us, and who has also put his seal on us and given us his Spirit in our hearts as a guarantee"—God's great benediction.

In this passage, we see the roles of the Godhead: the Father saying "Yes" to all His promises through His Son; Jesus who has anointed us and given us His Spirit; the Spirit who is the guarantee (of our inheritance: Ephesians 1:14).

Through the night:
In peace I will both lie down and sleep; for you alone, O LORD, make me dwell in safety.

PSALM 4:8

Our "Amen" means that we can be settled in the knowledge that God has established us; He's secured us. In that security, we can be at peace even if all around us is turmoil. We are—through Jesus—saying "Let it be so!" for God's glory.

After *Shalom*, I will either continue to sojourn through my day, praying through my moments and hours; or I will sleep. In either case, I am at peace, knowing: "By day the LORD commands his steadfast love, and at night his song is with me, a prayer to the God of my life" (Psalm 42:8).

"Truly God has listened; he has attended to the voice of my prayer."
Psalm 66:19

PATH MARKER

Consider ending your prayer time with the beautiful last "Amen" in the Bible: "He who testifies to these things says, 'Surely I am coming soon.' Amen. Come, Lord Jesus! The grace of the Lord Jesus be with all. Amen." (Revelation 22:20–21)

A Prayer of Shalom

Dear Jehovah-Shalom, Prince of Peace, and
Eternal Holy Spirit:

You are our only peace in this turbulent world. You are with me every step of my life's journey, hedging me in behind and before. My heart is tattered from the battle, but Your peace holds me together. This present darkness is not dark to You. I rest, knowing that You are awake. You are holding and guarding me. I am safe under Your wings. I have nothing to fear. *I will walk in the name of the LORD my God forever.*

I am in peace.

Amen and amen.

> *"Blessed be the LORD forever! Amen and Amen."*
> *Psalm 89:52*

PRAYER PASSAGES

While the earth remains, seedtime and harvest, cold and heat, summer and winter, day and night, shall not cease.
Genesis 8:22

The LORD bless you and keep you; the LORD make his face to shine upon you and be gracious to you; the LORD lift up his countenance upon you and give you peace.
Numbers 6:24–26

And now, O Lord GOD, you are God, and your words are true, and you have promised this good thing to your servant. Now therefore may it please you to bless the house of your servant, so that it may continue forever before you. For you, O Lord GOD, have spoken, and with your blessing shall the house of your servant be blessed forever.
2 Samuel 7:28–29

The LORD our God be with us, as he was with our fathers. May he not leave us or forsake us, that he may incline our hearts to him, to walk in all his ways and to keep his commandments, his statutes, and his rules, which he commanded our fathers. Let these words of mine, with which I have pleaded before the LORD, be near to the LORD our God day and night, and may he maintain the cause of his servant and the cause of his people Israel, as each day requires.
1 Kings 8:57–59

By morning and evening prayer we give glory to him who is the Alpha and the Omega , the first and the last; with him we must begin and end the day, begin and end the night, who is the beginning and the end, the first cause, and the last end.

MATTHEW HENRY

I cried aloud to the LORD, and he answered me from his holy hill. *Selah* I lay down and slept; I woke again, for the LORD sustained me.

Psalm 3:4–5

Salvation belongs to the LORD; your blessing be on your people! *Selah*

Psalm 3:8

Be angry, and do not sin; ponder in your own hearts on your beds, and be silent. *Selah*

Psalm 4:4

In peace I will both lie down and sleep; for you alone, O LORD, make me dwell in safety.

Psalm 4:8

You have given him his heart's desire and have not withheld the request of his lips. *Selah*

Psalm 21:2

The LORD is my shepherd; I shall not want. He makes me lie down in green pastures. He leads me beside still waters. He restores my soul. He leads me in paths of righteousness for his name's sake. Even though I walk through the valley of the shadow of death, I will fear no evil, for you are with me; your rod and your staff, they comfort me. You prepare a table before me in the presence of my enemies; you anoint my head with oil; my cup overflows. Surely goodness and mercy shall follow me all the days of my life, and I shall dwell in the house of the LORD forever.

Psalm 23

Grant to me above all things that can be desired, to rest in Thee, and in Thee to have my heart at peace. Thou art the true peace of the heart, Thou its only rest. . . . In this very peace, that is, in Thee, the One Chiefest Eternal Good, I will sleep and rest.

THOMAS À KEMPIS

Wait for the LORD; be strong, and let your heart take courage; wait for the LORD!
Psalm 27:14

May the LORD give strength to his people! May the LORD bless his people with peace!
Psalm 29:11

Be strong, and let your heart take courage, all you who wait for the LORD!
Psalm 31:24

You are a hiding place for me; you preserve me from trouble; you surround me with shouts of deliverance. *Selah*
Psalm 32:7

Turn away from evil and do good; seek peace and pursue it.
Psalm 34:14

Blessed be the LORD, the God of Israel, from everlasting to everlasting! Amen and Amen.
Psalm 41:13

By day the LORD commands his steadfast love, and at night his song is with me, a prayer to the God of my life.
Psalm 42:8

O my Strength, I will watch for you, for you, O God, are my fortress.
Psalm 55:9

Let me dwell in your tent forever! Let me take refuge under the shelter of your wings! *Selah*
Psalm 61:4

He who believes in God is not careful for the morrow, but labors joyfully and with a great heart. "For He giveth His beloved, as in sleep." They must work and watch, yet never be careful or anxious, but commit all to Him, and live in serene tranquility; and with a quiet heart, as one who sleeps sparely and quietly.

ELISABETH ELLIOT

On God rests my salvation and my glory; my mighty rock, my refuge is God. Trust in him at all times, O people; pour out your heart before him; God is a refuge for us. *Selah*
Psalm 62:7–8

All the earth worships you and sings praises to you; they sing praises to your name. *Selah*
Psalm 66:4

May God be gracious to us and bless us and make his face to shine upon us. *Selah*
Psalm 67:1

Let the nations be glad and sing for joy, for you judge the peoples with equity and guide the nations upon earth. *Selah* Let the peoples praise you, O God; let all the peoples praise you!
Psalm 67:4–5

Blessed be the Lord, who daily bears us up; God is our salvation. *Selah*
Psalm 68:19

May his name endure forever, his fame continue as long as the sun! May people be blessed in him, all nations call him blessed! Blessed be the LORD, the God of Israel, who alone does wondrous things. Blessed be his glorious name forever; may the whole earth be filled with his glory! Amen and Amen!
Psalm 72:17–19

My flesh and my heart may fail, but God is the strength of my heart and my portion forever.
Psalm 73:26

Lord, let Thy peace rule in our hearts . . . let thy peace keep our hearts and minds, and give comfort to us; and let the consolations of God, which are neither few nor small, be our strength and our song in the house of our pilgrimage.
MATTHEW HENRY

Yours is the day, yours also the night.
Psalm 74:16a

Blessed are those who dwell in your house, ever singing your praise! *Selah*
Psalm 84:4

O LORD God of hosts, hear my prayer; give ear, O God of Jacob! *Selah*
Psalm 84:8

Blessed be the LORD forever! Amen and Amen.
Psalm 89:52

Yes, the world is established; it shall never be moved.
Psalm 93:1c

Blessed be the LORD, the God of Israel, from everlasting to everlasting! And let all the people say, "Amen!" Praise the LORD!
Psalm 106:48

Not to us, O LORD, not to us, but to your name give glory, for the sake of your steadfast love and your faithfulness! Why should the nations say, "Where is their God?" Our God is in the heavens; he does all that he pleases.
Psalm 115:1–3

Your testimonies are my heritage forever, for they are the joy of my heart. I incline my heart to perform your statutes forever, to the end.
Psalm 119:111–12

The LORD is your keeper. . . . The LORD will keep you from all evil; he will keep your life.
Psalm 121:5a, 7

Glory be to the Father,
and to the Son,
And to the Holy Ghost;
As it was in the beginning,
is now, and ever shall be,
World without end.
Amen, Amen.

GLORIA PATRI

To live coram Deo *is to live one's entire life in the presence of God, under the authority of God, to the glory of God.*

R.C. SPROUL

196

It is in vain that you rise up early and go late to rest, eating the bread of anxious toil; for he gives to his beloved sleep.

Psalm 127:2

You keep him in perfect peace whose mind is stayed on you, because he trusts in you. Trust in the LORD forever, for the LORD GOD is an everlasting rock.

Isaiah 26:3–4

And the effect of righteousness will be peace, and the result of righteousness, quietness and trust forever. My people will abide in a peaceful habitation, in secure dwellings, and in quiet resting places.

Isaiah 32:17–18

Fear not, for I am with you; be not dismayed, for I am your God; I will strengthen you, I will help you, I will uphold you with my righteous right hand.

Isaiah 41:10

Thus says the LORD: "Stand by the roads, and look, and ask for the ancient paths, where the good way is; and walk in it, and find rest for your souls."

Jeremiah 6:16a

For I know the plans I have for you, declares the LORD, plans for welfare and not for evil, to give you a future and a hope. Then you will call upon me and come and pray to me, and I will hear you. You will seek me and find me, when you seek me with all your heart.

Jeremiah 29:11–13

We are like to Him with whom there is no past or future, with whom a day is as a thousand years, and a thousand years as one day, when we ... [do] our work in the great present, leaving both past and future to Him to whom they are ever present, and fearing nothing, because He is in our future, as much as He is in our past, as much as, and far more than, we can feel Him to be in our present. ... We walk without fear, full of hope and courage and strength to do His will, waiting for the endless good which He is always giving as fast as He can get us able to take it in.

GEORGE
MACDONALD

Come to me, all who labor and are heavy laden, and I will give you rest. Take my yoke upon you, and learn from me, for I am gentle and lowly in heart, and you will find rest for your souls. For my yoke is easy, and my burden is light.
Matthew 11:28–30

Take heart; it is I. Do not be afraid.
Mark 6:50b

Peace I leave with you; my peace I give to you. Not as the world gives do I give to you. Let not your hearts be troubled, neither let them be afraid.
John 14:27

I have said these things to you, that in me you may have peace. In the world you will have tribulation. But take heart; I have overcome the world.
John 16:33

For to set the mind on the flesh is death, but to set the mind on the Spirit is life and peace.
Romans 8:6

For from him and through him and to him are all things. To him be glory forever. Amen.
Romans 11:36

May the God of hope fill you with all joy and peace in believing, so that by the power of the Holy Spirit you may abound in hope.
Romans 15:13

May the God of peace be with you all. Amen.
Romans 15:33

O God, our help in ages past,
Our hope for years to come,
Our shelter from the stormy blast,
And our eternal home.
ISAAC WATTS

To the only wise God be glory forevermore
through Jesus Christ! Amen.
Romans 16:27

Therefore, my beloved brothers, be steadfast,
immovable, always abounding in the work of the
Lord, knowing that in the Lord your labor is not
in vain.
1 Corinthians 15:58

For all the promises of God find their Yes in
him. That is why it is through him that we
utter our Amen to God for his glory. And it is
God who establishes us with you in Christ, and
has anointed us, and who has also put his seal
on us and given us his Spirit in our hearts as a
guarantee.
2 Corinthians 1:20–22

Live in peace; and the God of love and peace will
be with you.
2 Corinthians 13:11b

Grace to you and peace from God our Father and
the Lord Jesus Christ, who gave himself for our
sins to deliver us from the present evil age, according to the will of our God and Father, to whom be
the glory forever and ever. Amen.
Galatians 1:3–5

But now in Christ Jesus you who once were far off
have been brought near by the blood of Christ.
For he himself is our peace.
Ephesians 2:13–14a

*Courage, then, and
patience! Courage for the
great sorrows of life, and
patience for the small ones.
And then when you have
laboriously accomplished
your daily task, go to sleep
in peace. God is awake.*

VICTOR HUGO

Now to him who is able to do far more abundantly than all that we ask or think, according to the power at work within us, to him be glory in the church and in Christ Jesus throughout all generations, forever and ever. Amen.
Ephesians 3:20–21

The peace of God, which surpasses all understanding, will guard your hearts and your minds in Christ Jesus.
Philippians 4:7

To our God and Father be glory forever and ever. Amen.
Philippians 4:20

And let the peace of Christ rule in your hearts, to which indeed you were called in one body. And be thankful.
Colossians 3:15

Now may the God of peace himself sanctify you completely, and may your whole spirit and soul and body be kept blameless at the coming of our Lord Jesus Christ. He who calls you is faithful; he will surely do it.
1 Thessalonians 5:23–24

Now may our Lord Jesus Christ himself, and God our Father, who loved us and gave us eternal comfort and good hope through grace, comfort your hearts and establish them in every good work and word.
2 Thessalonians 2:16–17

Now may the Lord of peace himself give you peace at all times in every way. The Lord be with you all.
2 Thessalonians 3:16

Lord Jesus Christ! here I am. Henceforth Thy love shall be the only home of my soul: in Thy love alone will I abide.

ANDREW MURRAY

To the King of the ages, immortal, invisible, the only God, be honor and glory forever and ever. Amen.
1 Timothy 1:17

But I am not ashamed, for I know whom I have believed, and I am convinced that he is able to guard until that Day what has been entrusted to me.
2 Timothy 1:12b

The Lord will rescue me from every evil deed and bring me safely into his heavenly kingdom. To him be the glory forever and ever. Amen.
2 Timothy 4:18

Waiting for our blessed hope, the appearing of the glory of our great God and Savior Jesus Christ.
Titus 2:13

Now may the God of peace who brought again from the dead our Lord Jesus, the great shepherd of the sheep, by the blood of the eternal covenant, equip you with everything good that you may do his will, working in us that which is pleasing in his sight, through Jesus Christ, to whom be glory forever and ever. Amen.
Hebrews 13:20–21

The wisdom from above is first pure, then peaceable, gentle, open to reason, full of mercy and good fruits, impartial and sincere. And a harvest of righteousness is sown in peace by those who make peace.
James 1:17–18

You also, be patient. Establish your hearts, for the coming of the Lord is at hand.
James 5:8

Good-night! Good-night!
Far flies the light;
But still God's love
Shall flame above,
Making all bright.
Good-night! Good-night!
VICTOR HUGO

To him belong glory and dominion forever and ever. Amen.

1 Peter 4:11c

Grow in the grace and knowledge of our Lord and Savior Jesus Christ. To him be the glory both now and to the day of eternity. Amen.

2 Peter 3:18

Grace, mercy, and peace will be with us, from God the Father and from Jesus Christ the Father's Son, in truth and love.

2 John 3

May mercy, peace, and love be multiplied to you.

Jude 2

Now to him who is able to keep you from stumbling and to present you blameless before the presence of his glory with great joy, to the only God, our Savior, through Jesus Christ our Lord, be glory, majesty, dominion, and authority, before all time and now and forever. Amen.

Jude 24–25

Amen! Blessing and glory and wisdom and thanksgiving and honor and power and might be to our God forever and ever! Amen.

Revelation 7:12

Behold, I am coming soon, bringing my recompense with me, to repay each one for what he has done. I am the Alpha and the Omega, the first and the last, the beginning and the end.

Revelation 22:12–13

Christ be beside me;
Christ be before me;
Christ be behind me;
King of my heart.
Christ be within me;
Christ be below me;
Christ be above me,
Never to part.

PATRICK OF
IRELAND

He who testifies to these things says, "Surely I am coming soon." Amen. Come, Lord Jesus! The grace of the Lord Jesus be with all. Amen.
Revelation 22:20–21

While I am a pilgrim here,
Let Thy love my spirit
cheer;
As my Guide, my Guard,
my Friend,
Lead me to my journey's
end.

JOHN NEWTON

Additional Verses

Additional Verses

Additional Verses

PART 3

RESOURCES

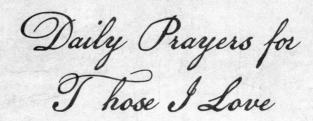

Daily Prayers for Those I Love

- I pray that we would love the Lord our God with all our hearts, souls, minds, and strength, and love our neighbors as we love ourselves. (Mark 12:30–31)

- I pray that we would guard our hearts with vigilance. (Proverbs 4:23)

- I pray that we would walk as children of light. (Ephesians 5:8)

- I pray that we would wear the armor of God. (Ephesians 6:10–20)

- I pray that we would number our days that we might gain a heart of wisdom. (Psalm 90:12)

- I pray that we would cast all our anxieties on God, knowing that He cares for us. (1 Peter 5:7)

- I pray that we would abide in Christ. (John 15:5)

- I pray that I would have no greater joy than to hear of my loved ones walking in Christ. (3 John 4)

PRAYER THEMES
A Month of Daily Prayers

THESE *PRAYER THEMES* focus on praying for your spouse, your family, or others. One topic is listed for each day of the month. Consider leaving this book or your own prayer notebook on your desk or kitchen counter or post a specific guide on your refrigerator or bathroom mirror to catch your attention and remind you to pray. Some people find it helpful to send themselves reminders via computer or smart phone calendar apps.

PRAYING EVERY DAY FOR THOSE I LOVE

1. I pray that they would love God, Jesus, and the Holy Spirit:

I love you, O LORD, my strength.
Psalm 18:1

[Jesus said:] You shall love the Lord your God with all your heart and with all your soul and with all your mind and with all your strength.
Mark 12:30

2. I pray that they would love others:

[Jesus said:] You shall love your neighbor as yourself.
Mark 12:31a

If God so loved us, we also ought to love one another.
1 John 4:11

3. I pray that they would resist Satan, and flee from sin, and that they would be eager to repent when sin is revealed:

Resist the devil, and he will flee from you.
James 4:7b

If we confess our sins, he is faithful and just to forgive us our sins and to cleanse us from all unrighteousness.
1 John 1:9

Are there any bound to us in the relations of life whose habits anyways are annoying and distasteful to us? Can we bear with them in love? . . . The examination will probably teach us to feel the infinite distance between us and our divine Ideal, and change censoriousness of others into prayer for ourselves.

HARRIET BEECHER STOWE

210

4. I pray that they would submit to discipline and correction:

Listen to advice and accept instruction, that you may gain wisdom in the future.
Proverbs 19:20

For the moment all discipline seems painful rather than pleasant, but later it yields the peaceful fruit of righteousness to those who have been trained by it.
Hebrews 12:11

5. I pray that they would be drawn to the Word and to prayer:

Open my eyes, that I may behold wondrous things out of your law. . . . Oh how I love your law! It is my meditation all the day.
Psalm 119:18, 97

Continue steadfastly in prayer, being watchful in it with thanksgiving.
Colossians 4:2

6. I pray that they would not love the world:

Do not be conformed to this world, but be transformed by the renewal of your mind, that by testing you may discern what is the will of God, what is good and acceptable and perfect.
Romans 12:2

Do not love the world or the things in the world. If anyone loves the world, the love of the Father is not in him.
I John 2:15

The Word of God is the only sure foundation for prayer. . . . Prayer depends on the Word of God.

JOHN CALVIN

7. I pray that they would resist temptation:

Abhor what is evil; hold fast to what is good.
Romans 12:9b

No temptation has overtaken you that is not common to man. God is faithful, and he will not let you be tempted beyond your ability.
1 Corinthians 10:13a

8. I pray that they would trust God with their future (education, career, ministry, marriage, etc.):

Trust in the LORD with all your heart, and do not lean on your own understanding. In all your ways acknowledge him, and he will make straight your paths.
Proverbs 3:5–6

For I know the plans I have for you, declares the LORD, plans for welfare and not for evil, to give you a future and a hope.
Jeremiah 29:11

9. I pray that they would be pure:

[Jesus said:] Blessed are the pure in heart, for they shall see God.
Matthew 5:8

Be diligent to be found by him without spot or blemish, and at peace.
2 Peter 3:14b

Stand still awhile, and seriously consider the noble end for which thou wast created, and for which God hath placed thee in this world! Thou wast not created for time and the creature, but for God and eternity, and to employ thyself with God and eternity.

GERHARD
TERSTEEGEN

10. I pray that they would know that they are precious to God:

The LORD your God is in your midst, a mighty one who will save; he will rejoice over you with gladness; he will quiet you by his love; he will exult over you with loud singing.
Zephaniah 3:17

See what kind of love the Father has given to us, that we should be called children of God; and so we are.
1 John 3:1a

11. I pray that they would be satisfied in God—that He would be their treasure:

One thing have I asked of the LORD, that will I seek after: that I may dwell in the house of the LORD all the days of my life.
Psalm 27:4a

[Jesus said:] For where your treasure is, there will your heart be also.
Luke 12:34

12. I pray that they would be true worshipers of God:

[Jesus said:] You shall worship the Lord your God, and him only shall you serve.
Luke 4:8b

[Jesus said:] God is spirit, and those who worship him must worship in spirit and truth.
John 4:24

Prayer and I are all one. Prayer is the soul's traffic with heaven. God comes down to us by his Spirit and we go up to him by prayer.

THOMAS WATSON

213

13. I pray that their lives would show the fruit of the Spirit:

But the fruit of the Spirit is love, joy, peace, patience, kindness, goodness, faithfulness, gentleness, self-control.
Galatians 5:22–23a

14. I pray that they would have godly influences in their lives and that they would be wise in choosing friends:

Whoever walks with the wise becomes wise, but the companion of fools will suffer harm.
Proverbs 13:20

Do not be deceived: "Bad company ruins good morals."
1 Corinthians 15:33

15. I pray that they would have servant hearts:

[Jesus said:] If anyone would be first, he must be last of all and servant of all.
Mark 9:35b

As each has received a gift, use it to serve one another, as good stewards.
1 Peter 4:10a

16. I pray that they would be peacemakers:

[Jesus said:] Blessed are the peacemakers, for they shall be called sons of God.
Matthew 5:9

Christ's love will do more than restrain us from evil. It will lead us also into good. It will do more than prevent us from living unto ourselves. It will also lead us to live unto him.

J. GRESHAM MACHEN

A harvest of righteousness is sown in peace by those who make peace.
James 3:18

17. I pray that they would follow the narrow path:

You make known to me the path of life; in your presence there is fullness of joy; at your right hand are pleasures forevermore.
Psalm 16:11

[Jesus said:] Enter by the narrow gate. For the gate is wide and the way is easy that leads to destruction, and those who enter by it are many. For the gate is narrow and the way is hard that leads to life, and those who find it are few.
Matthew 7:13–14

18. I pray that they would be self-disciplined (in thoughts, words, actions, money, eating, drinking, what they view, and what they listen to):

A man without self-control is like a city broken into and left without walls.
Proverbs 25:28

I discipline my body and keep it under control.
1 Corinthians 9:27a

19. I pray that they would grow in spiritual discernment:

Be not wise in your own eyes; fear the LORD, and turn away from evil.
Proverbs 3:7

To spend our lives so as to be only journeying towards heaven, is the way to be free from bondage.

JONATHAN
EDWARDS

[Jesus said:] Man shall not live by bread alone, but by every word that comes from the mouth of God.
Matthew 4:4b

20. I pray that they would live in joy:

The joy of the LORD is your strength.
Nehemiah 8:10b

I will turn their mourning into joy; I will comfort them, and give them gladness for sorrow.
Jeremiah 31:13b

21. I pray that they would be doers of the Word and not hearers only:

Be doers of the word, and not hearers only.
James 1:22a

Little children, let us not love in word or talk but in deed and in truth.
1 John 3:18

22. I pray that they would be content:

I have learned in whatever situation I am to be content.
Philippians 4:11b

God will supply every need of yours according to his riches in glory in Christ Jesus.
Philippians 4:19

23. I pray that they would not be anxious:

Do not be anxious about anything, but in everything by prayer and supplication with thanksgiving let your requests be made known to God.
Philippians 4:6

Thou has willed it that through labour and pain I should walk the upward way; be Thou then my fellow traveller as I go.

JOHN BAILLIE

[Cast] all your anxieties on him, because he cares for you.
1 Peter 5:7

24. I pray that they would be forgiving and not hold grudges:

Be kind to one another, tenderhearted, forgiving one another, as God in Christ forgave you.
Ephesians 4:32

[Bear] with one another and, if one has a complaint against another, forgiving each other; as the Lord has forgiven you, so you also must forgive.
Colossians 3:13

25. I pray that they would not be proud:

Do nothing from selfish ambition or conceit, but in humility count others more significant than yourselves. Let each of you look not only to his own interests, but also to the interests of others.
Philippians 2:3–4

God opposes the proud, but gives grace to the humble.
James 4:6b

26. I pray that they would desire inward beauty and excellent character in themselves and others:

Man looks on the outward appearance, but the Lord looks on the heart.
1 Samuel 16:7b

What the Christian used to be is altogether the least important thing about him. What he is yet to be is all that should concern him. He may occasionally . . . remember to his own shame the life he once lived; but that should only be a quick glance; it is never to be a fixed gaze. Our long permanent look is on God and the glory that shall be revealed.

A. W. TOZER

Let your adorning be the hidden person of the heart with the imperishable beauty of a gentle and quiet spirit, which in God's sight is very precious.
1 Peter 3:4

27. I pray that they would be honest:

Truthful lips endure forever, but a lying tongue is but for a moment.
Proverbs 12:19

The getting of treasures by a lying tongue is a fleeting vapor and a snare of death.
Proverbs 21:6

28. I pray that they would be teachable:

Whoever loves discipline loves knowledge, but he who hates reproof is stupid.
Proverbs 12:1

Whoever ignores instruction despises himself, but he who listens to reproof gains intelligence.
Proverbs 15:32–33

29. I pray that they would persevere under trials:

Count it all joy, my brothers, when you meet trials of various kinds, for you know that the testing of your faith produces steadfastness.
James 1:2–3

Blessed is the man who remains steadfast under trial, for when he has stood the test he will receive

Therefore, it behoves us to ask with so much the greater care, that he would increase our hope when it is small, awaken it when it is dormant, confirm it when it is wavering, strengthen it when it is weak, and that he would even raise it up when it is overthrown.

JOHN CALVIN

the crown of life, which God has promised to
those who love him.

James 1:12

30. I pray that they would be spiritually strong:

Be strong in the Lord and in the strength of his
might. Put on the whole armor of God, that you
may be able to stand against the schemes of the devil.

Ephesians 6:10–11

Be sober-minded; be watchful. Your adversary the
devil prowls around like a roaring lion, seeking
someone to devour.

1 Peter 5:8

31. I pray that they would abide in Christ:

[Jesus said:] As the Father has loved me, so have I
loved you. Abide in my love.

John 15:9

No one who abides in him keeps on sinning; no
one who keeps on sinning has either seen him or
known him.

1 John 3:6

*O Thou by whom we come
to God,
The Life, the Truth, the
Way!
The path of prayer Thyself
hast trod;
Lord, teach us how to
pray.*

JAMES
MONTGOMERY

PRAYING EVERY DAY FOR MY HUSBAND

1. I pray that he would love God above all:

[Jesus said:] You shall love the Lord your God with all your heart and with all your soul and with all your mind and with all your strength. . . . You shall love your neighbor as yourself.

Mark 12:30–31

Walk in a manner worthy of the calling to which you have been called.

Ephesians 4:1b

2. I pray that he would be wise:

Do not be conformed to this world, but be transformed by the renewal of your mind.

Romans 12:2a

If any of you lacks wisdom, let him ask God, who gives generously . . . and it will be given him.

James 1:5

3. I pray that he would bear fruit:

He is like a tree planted by streams of water that yields its fruit in its season, and its leaf does not wither. In all that he does, he prospers.

Psalm 1:3

[Jesus said:] Whoever abides in me and I in him, he it is that bears much fruit, for apart from me you can do nothing.
John 15:5b

Walk in a manner worthy of the Lord, fully pleasing to him, bearing fruit in every good work.
Colossians 1:10a

4. I pray that he would be committed to our marriage:

So guard yourselves in your spirit, and let none of you be faithless to the wife of your youth.
Malachi 2:15b

Husbands, love your wives, as Christ loved the church and gave himself up for her.
Ephesians 5:25

5. I pray for him in trials:

Count it all joy . . . when you meet trials of various kinds, for you know that the testing of your faith produces steadfastness.
James 1:2–3

The Lord knows how to rescue the godly from trials.
2 Peter 2:9a

6. I pray that he would have integrity:

The integrity of the upright guides them, but the crookedness of the treacherous destroys them.
Proverbs 11:3

A good name is to be chosen rather than great riches.
Proverbs 22:1a

7. I pray that he would be hope-filled:

The steadfast love of the LORD never ceases; his mercies never come to an end; they are new every morning; great is your faithfulness.
Lamentations 3:22–23

Rejoice in hope, be patient in tribulation, be constant in prayer.
Romans 12:12

8. I pray for his priorities:

[Jesus said:] Seek first the kingdom of God and his righteousness, and all these things will be added to you.
Matthew 6:33

Be watchful, stand firm in the faith, act like men, be strong. Let all that you do be done in love.
1 Corinthians 16:13–14

9. I pray for his fathering:

You shall teach them diligently to your children.
Deuteronomy 6:7a

With upright heart he shepherded them and guided them with his skillful hand.
Psalm 78:72

Fathers, do not provoke your children to anger, but bring them up in the discipline and instruction of the Lord.
Ephesians 6:4

10. I pray that I would be his encourager:

An excellent wife is the crown of her husband, but she who brings shame is like rottenness in his bones.
Proverbs 12:4

He who finds a wife finds a good thing and obtains favor from the LORD.
Proverbs 18:22

It is better to live in a corner of the housetop than in a house shared with a quarrelsome wife.
Proverbs 21:9

The heart of her husband trusts in her, and he will have no lack of gain. She does him good, and not harm, all the days of her life.
Proverbs 31:11–12

11. I pray for his joy and his anxieties:

The joy of the LORD is your strength.
Nehemiah 8:10b

Rejoice in the Lord always; again I will say, rejoice . . . do not be anxious about anything, but in everything by prayer and supplication with thanksgiving let your requests be made known to God.
Philippians 4:4, 6

12. I pray for his faith:

[Jesus said:] O you of little faith, why did you doubt?
Matthew 14:31b

Without faith it is impossible to please him, for whoever would draw near to God must believe that he exists and that he rewards those who seek him.
Hebrews 11:6

13. I pray for his leadership and my responsiveness:

The head of every man is Christ, the head of a wife is her husband, and the head of Christ is God.
1 Corinthians 11:3

For the husband is the head of the wife even as Christ is the head of the church, his body, and is himself its Savior.
Ephesians 5:23

14. I pray for his tongue:

Set a guard, O LORD, over my mouth.
Psalm 141:3a

[Jesus said:] For out of the abundance of the heart the mouth speaks.
Matthew 12:34b

15. I pray for his repentance:

Search me, O God, and know my heart! Try me and know my thoughts! And see if there be any grievous way in me.
Psalm 139:23–24a

If we confess our sins, he is faithful and just to forgive us our sins and to cleanse us from all unrighteousness.
1 John 1:9

16. I pray for his battles with temptation:

Abhor what is evil; hold fast to what is good.
Romans 12:9b

No temptation has overtaken you that is not common to man. God is faithful, and he will not let you be tempted beyond your ability.
1 Corinthians 10:13a

17. I pray that he would be obedient to God:

Be careful to obey all these words that I command you, that it may go well with you and with your children after you forever, when you do what is good and right in the sight of the LORD your God.
Deuteronomy 12:28

18. I pray for his thought life:

Whatever is true, whatever is honorable, whatever is just, whatever is pure, whatever is lovely, whatever is commendable, if there is any excellence, if there is anything worthy of praise, think about these things.
Philippians 4:8

19. I pray that he would abide in Christ:

[Jesus said:] Come to me, all who labor and are heavy laden, and I will give you rest.
Matthew 11:28

Whoever says he abides in him ought to walk in the same way in which he walked.
1 John 2:6

20. I pray that he would be content:

I have learned in whatever situation I am to be content.
Philippians 4:11b

But godliness with contentment is great gain.
1 Timothy 6:6

21. I pray for his emotions:

Why are you cast down, O my soul, and why are you in turmoil within me? Hope in God; for I shall again praise him, my salvation and my God.
Psalm 42:11

Whoever is slow to anger is better than the mighty.
Proverbs 16:32a

22. I pray that he would be brave:

Be strong and courageous. Do not be frightened . . . for the LORD . . . is with you.
Joshua 1:9

Fear not, for I am with you; be not dismayed, for I am your God; I will strengthen you, I will help you, I will uphold you with my righteous right hand.
Isaiah 41:10

23. I pray for his sexual purity:

I will not set before my eyes anything that is worthless.
Psalm 101:3a

[Jesus said:] Blessed are the pure in heart, for they shall see God.
Matthew 5:8

24. I pray for his work:

Whatever you do, in word or deed, do everything in the name of the Lord Jesus.
Colossians 3:17a

Whatever you do, work heartily, as for the Lord and not for men.
Colossians 3:23

25. I pray for him to have peace regarding finances:

[Jesus said:] And do not seek what you are to eat and what you are to drink, nor be worried . . . your Father knows that you need them. Instead, seek his kingdom, and these things will be added to you.
Luke 12:29, 30b–31

Keep your life free from love of money.
Hebrews 13:5a

26. I pray for our marriage bed:

Let your fountain be blessed, and rejoice in the wife of your youth. . . . Let her breasts fill you at all times with delight; be intoxicated always in her love.
Proverbs 5:18, 19b

Do not deprive one another, except perhaps by agreement for a limited time, that you may devote yourselves to prayer.
1 Corinthians 7:5a

Let marriage be held in honor among all, and let the marriage bed be undefiled.
Hebrews 13:4a

27. I pray for his aging:

They are planted in the house of the LORD; they flourish in the courts of our God. They still bear fruit in old age.
Psalm 92:13–14a

Grandchildren are the crown of the aged, and the glory of children is their fathers.
Proverbs 17:6

To your old age I am he, and to gray hairs I will carry you. I have made, and I will bear; I will carry and will save.
Isaiah 46:4

28. I pray for his friendships:

Iron sharpens iron, and one man sharpens another.
Proverbs 27:17

Do not be deceived: "Bad company ruins good morals."
1 Corinthians 15:33

29. I pray that he would be a man of peace:

You keep him in perfect peace whose mind is stayed on you, because he trusts in you.
Isaiah 26:3

[Jesus said:] Blessed are the peacemakers, for they shall be called sons of God.
Matthew 5:9

30. I pray that he would be a man of the Word and of prayer:

Open my eyes, that I may behold wondrous things out of your law. . . . Oh how I love your law! It is my meditation all the day.
Psalm 119:18, 97

Let the word of Christ dwell in you richly, teaching and admonishing one another in all wisdom, singing psalms and hymns and spiritual songs, with thankfulness in your hearts to God.
Colossians 3:16

Continue steadfastly in prayer, being watchful in it with thanksgiving.
Colossians 4:2

31. I pray that he would live in joy:

The joy of the Lord is your strength.
Nehemiah 8:10b

I will turn their mourning into joy; I will comfort them, and give them gladness for sorrow.
Jeremiah 31:13b

PRAYING EVERY DAY FOR MY WIFE

1. I pray that she would love God above all:

[Jesus said:] You shall love the Lord your God with all your heart and with all your soul and with all your mind and with all your strength. . . . You shall love your neighbor as yourself.
Mark 12:30–31

Walk in a manner worthy of the calling to which you have been called.
Ephesians 4:1b

2. I pray that she would be wise:

The fear of the Lord is the beginning of knowledge.
Proverbs 1:7a

She opens her mouth with wisdom, and the teaching of kindness is on her tongue.
Proverbs 31:26

If any of you lacks wisdom, let him ask God, who gives generously . . . and it will be given him.
James 1:5

3. I pray that she would bear fruit:

Give her of the fruit of her hands, and let her works praise her in the gates.
Proverbs 31:31

[Jesus said:] Whoever abides in me and I in him, he it is that bears much fruit, for apart from me you can do nothing.
John 15:5b

Walk in a manner worthy of the Lord, fully pleasing to him, bearing fruit in every good work.
Colossians 1:10a

4. I pray that I would lead well and that she would respond gladly to my leadership:

As the church submits to Christ, so also wives should submit in everything to their husbands.
Ephesians 5:24

Wives, submit to your husbands, as is fitting in the Lord.
Colossians 3:18

Wives, be subject to your own husbands, so that even if some do not obey the word, they may be won without a word by the conduct of their wives, when they see your respectful and pure conduct.
1 Peter 3:1–2

5. I pray for her in trials:

Count it all joy . . . when you meet trials of various kinds, for you know that the testing of your faith produces steadfastness.
James 1:2–3

The Lord knows how to rescue the godly from trials.
2 Peter 2:9a

6. I pray that I would love her sacrificially:

Love is patient and kind; love does not envy or boast; it is not arrogant or rude. It does not insist on its own way; it is not irritable or resentful . . . Love bears all things, believes all things, hopes all things, endures all things. Love never ends.
1 Corinthians 13:4–5, 7–8a

Husbands, love your wives, as Christ loved the church and gave himself up for her.
Ephesians 5:25

7. I pray that she would be hope-filled:

The steadfast love of the LORD never ceases; his mercies never come to an end; they are new every morning; great is your faithfulness.
Lamentations 3:22–23

Rejoice in hope, be patient in tribulation, be constant in prayer.
Romans 12:12

8. I pray for her priorities:

She looks well to the ways of her household and does not eat the bread of idleness.
Proverbs 31:27

[Jesus said:] Seek first the kingdom of God and his righteousness, and all these things will be added to you.
Matthew 6:33

9. I pray for her mothering:

You shall teach them diligently to your children.
Deuteronomy 6:7a

May you see your children's children.
Psalm 128:6a

Her children rise up and call her blessed.
Proverbs 31:28a

Bring [your children] up in the discipline and
instruction of the Lord.
Ephesians 6:4

10. I pray that she would be loving:

Love is patient and kind; love does not envy or
boast; it is not arrogant or rude. It does not insist
on its own way; it is not irritable or resentful. . . .
Love bears all things, believes all things, hopes all
things, endures all things. Love never ends.
1 Corinthians 13:4–5, 7–8a

11. I pray that she would be joy-filled:

The joy of the LORD is your strength.
Nehemiah 8:10b

Strength and dignity are her clothing, and she
laughs at the time to come.
Proverbs 31:25

Rejoice in the Lord always. . . . Do not be anxious
about anything, but in everything by prayer and
supplication with thanksgiving let your requests
be made known to God.
Philippians 4:4–6

12. I pray for her faith:

[Jesus said:] O you of little faith, why did you doubt?
Matthew 14:31b

Without faith it is impossible to please him, for whoever would draw near to God must believe that he exists and that he rewards those who seek him.
Hebrews 11:6

13. I pray for her patience:

Put on then, as God's chosen ones, holy and beloved, compassionate hearts, kindness, humility, meekness, and patience.
Colossians 3:12

Admonish the idle, encourage the fainthearted, help the weak, be patient with them all.
1 Thessalonians 5:14

14. I pray for her tongue:

Set a guard, O LORD, over my mouth.
Psalm 141:3

She opens her mouth with wisdom, and the teaching of kindness is on her tongue.
Proverbs 31:26

[Jesus said:] For out of the abundance of the heart the mouth speaks.
Matthew 12:34b

15. I pray for her repentance:

Search me, O God, and know my heart! Try me and know my thoughts! And see if there be any grievous way in me.
Psalm 139:23–24a

If we confess our sins, he is faithful and just to forgive us our sins and to cleanse us from all unrighteousness.
1 John 1:9

16. I pray for her battles with temptation:

Abhor what is evil; hold fast to what is good.
Romans 12:9b

No temptation has overtaken you that is not common to man. God is faithful, and he will not let you be tempted beyond your ability.
1 Corinthians 10:13a

17. I pray that she would be obedient to God:

Be careful to obey all these words that I command you, that it may go well with you and with your children after you forever, when you do what is good and right in the sight of the Lord your God.
Deuteronomy 12:28

18. I pray for her sense of modesty:

Like a gold ring in a pig's snout is a beautiful woman without discretion.
Proverbs 11:22

Women should adorn themselves in respectable apparel, with modesty and self-control.
1 Timothy 2:9a

19. I pray that she would abide in Christ:

[Jesus said:] Come to me, all who labor and are heavy laden, and I will give you rest.
Matthew 11:28

Whoever says he abides in him ought to walk in the same way in which he walked.
1 John 2:6

20. I pray for her self-acceptance and desire for inner beauty:

Man looks on the outward appearance, but the Lord looks on the heart.
1 Samuel 16:7b

Charm is deceitful, and beauty is vain, but a woman who fears the LORD is to be praised.
Proverbs 31:30

Let your adorning be the hidden person of the heart.
1 Peter 3:4a

21. I pray for her emotions:

Why are you cast down, O my soul, and why are you in turmoil within me? Hope in God; for I shall again praise him, my salvation and my God.
Psalm 42:11

Whoever is slow to anger is better than the mighty.
Proverbs 16:32a

22. I pray that she would be brave:

When I am afraid, I put my trust in you.
Psalm 56:3

Fear not, for I am with you; be not dismayed, for I
am your God; I will strengthen you, I will help you,
I will uphold you with my righteous right hand.
Isaiah 41:10

23. I pray for her purity:

I will not set before my eyes anything that is
worthless.
Psalm 101:3

[Jesus said:] Blessed are the pure in heart, for they
shall see God.
Matthew 5:8

24. I pray for her work:

She looks well to the ways of her household and
does not eat the bread of idleness.
Proverbs 31:27

Whatever you do, in word or deed, do everything
in the name of the Lord Jesus.
Colossians 3:17a

Whatever you do, work heartily, as for the Lord
and not for men.
Colossians 3:23

25. I pray for her to have peace regarding finances:

[Jesus said:] And do not seek what you are to eat and what you are to drink, nor be worried.
Luke 12:29

Keep your life free from love of money, and be content with what you have, for he has said, "I will never leave you nor forsake you."
Hebrews 13:5

26. I pray for our marriage bed:

Let your fountain be blessed, and rejoice in the wife of your youth. . . . Let her breasts fill you at all times with delight; be intoxicated always in her love.
Proverbs 5:18, 19b

Do not deprive one another, except perhaps by agreement for a limited time, that you may devote yourselves to prayer.
1 Corinthians 7:5a

Let marriage be held in honor among all, and let the marriage bed be undefiled.
Hebrews 13:4a

27. I pray for her aging:

[The righteous] are planted in the house of the LORD; they flourish in the courts of our God. They still bear fruit in old age.
Psalm 92:13–14a

Gray hair is a crown of glory; it is gained in a righteous life.
Proverbs 16:31

Grandchildren are the crown of the aged, and the glory of children is their fathers.
Proverbs 17:6

[God promises:] "To your old age I am he, and to gray hairs I will carry you. I have made, and I will bear; I will carry and will save."
Isaiah 46:4

28 I pray for her friendships:

Whoever walks with the wise becomes wise, but the companion of fools will suffer harm.
Proverbs 13:20

Do not be deceived: "Bad company ruins good morals."
1 Corinthians 15:33

29. I pray for her peace:

You keep him in perfect peace whose mind is stayed on you, because he trusts in you.
Isaiah 26:3

[Jesus said:] Blessed are the peacemakers, for they shall be called sons of God.
Matthew 5:9

Let the peace of Christ rule in your hearts, to which indeed you were called in one body. And be thankful.
Colossians 3:15

30. I pray that she would be a woman of the Word and of prayer:

Open my eyes, that I may behold wondrous things out of your law. . . . Oh how I love your law! It is my meditation all the day.
Psalm 119:18, 97

Let the word of Christ dwell in you richly, teaching and admonishing one another in all wisdom, singing psalms and hymns and spiritual songs, with thankfulness in your hearts to God.
Colossians 3:16

Continue steadfastly in prayer, being watchful in it with thanksgiving.
Colossians 4:2

31. I pray that she would live in joy:

The joy of the LORD is your strength.
Nehemiah 8:10b

I will turn their mourning into joy; I will comfort them, and give them gladness for sorrow.
Jeremiah 31:13b

PRAYER PLANNING

Making a Prayer Notebook

FOR YEARS I longed for a simple tool that would help me to organize my prayer concerns and keep a record of where I'd been in prayer. Eventually I developed a prayer notebook that has served as a compass for my prayer journey and a travel journal of where I've been. The following forms are part of this notebook. You may write in them here or print them out to make your own customizable prayer journal.

MAKING YOUR OWN NOTEBOOK

Making Prayer PathWay notebooks can be a fun, creative group or family project. As you set out, you may find these forms and resources helpful:

Forms
- My Weekly Prayer Planner
- PRAYERS Day Trip
- Daily Prayer Lists
- I'm Praying For
- Additional Verses (starting on page 57)

241

Resources
- Some Names of God (page 34)
- The "I AM" Statements of Christ (page 34)
- God Is . . . (pages 36–37)
- Prayer Themes: A Month of Daily Prayers (starting on page 209)

Don't feel that you need to use every form or use them in the way I will describe in the next section. You could use a binder that allows you to add or remove sections as your personal prayer path changes. Or you could skip my forms and simply divide a notebook or journal into sections for the various steps of Prayer PathWay.

My own preference is to have two different binders. One is for the steps of Prayer PathWay, with a divider for each of the seven steps and pages full of verse and quotes that encourage my praying. The other one is my prayer planner, with a divider for my weekly prayer plan, a divider for each day of the week (with that day's prayer list and prayer requests), a divider for a month of daily prayer themes, a divider for extra forms, and a divider for miscellaneous things—because there are always miscellaneous things! These two binders can easily be combined into one, thicker binder.

And now, go, write it before them on a tablet and inscribe it in a book, that it may be for the time to come as a witness forever.

ISAIAH 30:8

Whatever you do, please use your Bible as your main prayer book! Surely, leaving behind a ragged, torn old Bible at the end of your life will be the best testimony of where you've been and Who has been with you. Using different ink colors for notes and symbols can make your Bible something of a piece of personal artwork. (Some people are uncomfortable with actually marking up their Bibles. If that's the case for you, sticky notes or flags are great for making comments, recording dates, and highlighting significant verses.)

USING THE PRAYER PATHWAY FORMS

Step 1

Fill out the Weekly Prayer Planner form. Don't rush this process. Prayerfully think of people, groups, ministries, and others for whom you would like to pray. Revise your chart until you feel satisfied with your plan. I find it helpful to use different colors of ink to designate different prayer groups (e.g., red for my own family, green for extended family, blue for friends, pink for missionaries, black for church and other ministries). If you've never done a list like this before, start small—you may add to it in the future!

Step 2

Transfer each day's list to that day's Prayer List form and place it behind the proper divider for the day of the week.

Step 3

If you'd like to record prayer needs, use the I'm Praying For form. General, ongoing prayer items may be listed in the "What I'm Praying" section. Prayer requests and answers to prayer may be listed on those pages, as well. Place these behind the daily Prayer List to which it applies. Photocopy and add additional pages as necessary.

For example, if you list your grandparents on your Weekly Prayer Planner in the Monday column, transfer their names to Monday's Prayer List for Monday. Then place their names on an I'm Praying For form, along with requests you'd like to remember to pray for them. Place that sheet after the daily prayer list.

A word of caution! If filling out forms will cause you to get distracted from praying—don't use them! They're meant to be an encouragement to your prayer discipline—not another item on your to-do list.

And one other word of caution. If you decide to record personal information and prayer requests about yourself or others, please don't leave your notebook where others can read it or where you could possibly misplace it.

"Pray without ceasing."
1 Thessalonians 5:17

My Weekly Prayer Planner

Sunday	Monday	Tuesday	Wednesday	Thursday	Friday	Saturday

My Weekly Prayer Planner

Sunday	Monday	Tuesday	Wednesday	Thursday	Friday	Saturday

PRAYERS Day Trip

_____ / _____ / _____

PRAISE ....

....

....

REPENT ....

....

....

ASK ....

....

....

YIELD ....

....

....

EXPRESS THANKS ....

....

....

REJOICE ....

....

....

SHALOM. ....

....

....

PRAYERS Day Trip

_____ / _____ / _____

PRAISE

REPENT

ASK

YIELD

EXPRESS THANKS

REJOICE

SHALOM.

Sunday's Prayer List

Sunday's Prayer List

I'm praying for:

What I'm praying:

I'm praying for:

What I'm praying:

Monday's Prayer List

Monday's Prayer List

I'm praying for:

What I'm praying:

I'm praying for:

What I'm praying:

Tuesday's Prayer List

Tuesday's Prayer List

I'm praying for:

What I'm praying:

I'm praying for:

What I'm praying:

Wednesday's Prayer List

Wednesday's Prayer List

I'm praying for:

What I'm praying:

I'm praying for:

What I'm praying:

Thursday's Prayer List

Thursday's Prayer List

I'm praying for:

What I'm praying:

I'm praying for:

What I'm praying:

Friday's Prayer List

Friday's Prayer List

I'm praying for:

What I'm praying:

I'm praying for:

What I'm praying:

Saturday's Prayer List

Saturday's Prayer List

I'm praying for:

What I'm praying:

I'm praying for:

What I'm praying:

INDEX OF
QUOTATIONS

I HAVE SELECTED quotations that underscore biblical truths and inspire the heart. While I am not endorsing all the theological convictions, denominational affiliations, or lifestyle expressions of those I have quoted, it is my sincere hope that the wise words of these imperfect but inspiring sages will bolster your faith and fuel your prayers. The books that I particularly love and would commend to you are marked with ❦. I also wholeheartedly recommend the English Standard Version of the Bible, published by Crossway, which I have quoted throughout.

Many of these sources are in the public domain and can be found online. Great effort has been made to ensure that the quotations are correctly worded and attributed, and early or original sources have been found, where possible. Page numbers are to the left; citations are on the right. Where a hymn's title and first line are identical, only the publication year is given.

Ambrose of Milan

43   *To Thee our morning song of praise* . . . Ambrose of Milan (337–397), "O Trinity of Blessed Light," trans. John Chandler, 1851.

Anonymous

124   *Trust the past to the mercy of God* . . . Quoted by Martin H. Manser, ed., *The Westminster Collection of Christian Quotations* (Louisville:

Westminster John Knox Press, 2001), 303. This quotation is commonly attributed to Augustine of Hippo.

Anselm of Canterbury

21 *This debt was so great* . . . Anselm (1033–1109), *Works of St. Anselm*, trans. Sidney Norton Deane, 1903, available on *Sacred Texts*, accessed Sept. 26, 2016, http://www.sacred-texts.com/chr/ans/ans118.htm.

Augustine of Hippo

35 *Great are You, O Lord* . . . Temple Scott, ed., *Confessions of Saint Augustine*, trans. E. B. Pusey ❦ (New York: E. P. Dutton and Co., 1900), 1. The wording has been modernized.

41 *You awaken us to delight in Your praise* . . . Ibid., 1. The wording has been modernized.

164 *This is the happy life* . . . Ibid., 255.

180 *There is a joy which is not given to the ungodly* . . . Ibid.

Baillie, John

15 *The Christian way whereon I walk* . . . John Baillie, *A Diary of Private Prayer* (New York: Charles Scribner's Sons, 1949), 25.

71 *Let me face what Thou dost send* . . . Ibid., 85.

216 *Thou has willed it that through labour and pain I should walk* . . . Ibid.

Bakker, Frans

153 *True thankfulness always glorifies God.* Frans Bakker, *Praying Always* (Edinburgh: Banner of Truth Trust, 1987), 24.

Baxter, J. Sidlow

112 *Men may spurn our appeals* . . . Quoted in Charlie Jones and Bob Kelly, *The Tremendous Power of Prayer* (West Monroe: Howard Publishing Company, 2000), 46.

Beecher, Henry Ward

153 *The unthankful heart discovers no mercies* . . . Henry Ward Beecher, *Life Thoughts* (New York: Sheldon and Co., 1860), 116.

Bonar, Andrew

137 *God may not give us an easy journey* . . . Quoted in Delavan L. Pierson, ed., *The Northfield Year-book for Each New Day* (New York: Fleming H. Revell, Co., 1896), 352.

Bonar, Horatius

126 *Thy way, not mine, O Lord . . .* 1857.

Bonhoeffer, Dietrich

39 *If we are to pray aright . . .* Dietrich Bonhoeffer, *Psalms* (Minneapolis: Augsburg Fortress, 1970), 15.

81 *In confession the light of the Gospel breaks into the darkness . . .* Dietrich Bonhoeffer, *Life Together* ❦ (New York: HarperCollins, 1954), 112.

101 *Intercession means no more . . .* Ibid., 86.

154 *Only he who gives thanks for little things . . .* Ibid., 29.

Book of Common Prayer, The

63 *Almighty God, unto whom all hearts be open . . .* Thomas Cranmer, *The Book of Common Prayer*, 1662. Spelling and punctuation have been modernized.

Booth, Catherine

128 *Whatever the particular call is . . .* Quoted in Frederick St. George De Lautour Booth-Tucker, *The Life of Catherine Booth, Vol. II* (London: The Salvation Army, n.d.), 410–11.

Bounds, E. M.

113 *Prayer breaks all bars . . .* Harold Chadwick, ed., *E. M. Bounds: Classic Collection of Prayer* (Alachua: Bridge-Logos, 2001), 30.

Bowman, Hetty

136 *When once our hearts are yielded to His service . . .* Hetty Bowman, *Thoughts from the Christian Life* (London: William Hunt & Co., 1872), 10.

Brontë, Charlotte

52 *We know that God is everywhere . . .* Charlotte Brontë, *Jane Eyre, Life and Works of Charlotte Brontë and Her Sisters, Vol. 1* (London: Smith, Elder & Co., 1872), 344.

Brooks, Phillips

104 *O Lord, I do not pray for tasks equal to my strength . . .* Quoted in Horton Davies, ed., *The Communion of Saints: Prayers of the Famous* (Grand Rapids: William B. Eerdmans Publishing Company, 1990), 32.

Bunyan, John

77 *Take heed of little sins.* John Bunyan, *The Works of That Eminent Servant of Christ, John Bunyan, Vol. 2* (Philadelphia: John Locken, 1832), 96.

129 *What God says is best, is best . . .* John Bunyan, *The Pilgrim's Progress* ❦ (London: The Religious Tract Society, 1799), 88.

134 *Conversion is not the smooth, easy-going process some men seem to think.* Quoted in John Brown, *John Bunyan: His Life, Times and Work* (London: Wm. Isbister, Ltd., 1886), 380.

Bushnell, Horace

135 *Take your burdens . . .* Horace Bushnell, *The New Life* (London: Alexander Strahan Publisher, 1866), 15.

Calvin, John

82 *Our sins are like a wall . . .* John Calvin, *Commentaries on the Psalms 1–35,* trans. John King (Altenmünster, Germany: JazzyBee Verlag, 2012). Kindle edition.

178 *There is not one blade of grass . . .* Quoted in William J. Bouwsma, *John Calvin: A Sixteenth Century Portrait* (Oxford: Oxford University Press, 1988), 134–35.

211 *The Word of God is the only sure foundation for prayer.* John Calvin, *The Necessity of Reforming the Church,* trans. H. Beveridge (London: W. H. Dalton, 1843), 61.

218 *Therefore, it behooves us to ask with so much the greater care . . .* Calvin, *Commentaries on the Psalms 1–35.* Kindle edition.

Carmichael, Amy

110 *That which I know not . . .* Amy Carmichael, *If* ❦ (Grand Rapids: Zondervan, 1965), no page numbers.

167 *Joys are always on their way . . .* Amy Carmichael, *Edges of His Ways* (Fort Washington, PA: CLC Publications, 1955), 82.

Chambers, Oswald

129 *God does not give us overcoming life . . .* Oswald Chambers, "The Teaching of Adversity," *My Utmost for His Highest,* August 2, 2016, accessed Sept. 19, 2016, http://utmost.org/the-teaching-of-adversity/.

136 *God never gives strength for tomorrow . . .* Ibid.

Fry, Elizabeth

137 *Lord, be pleased to help* . . . Quoted in Edith Deen, ed., *Great Women of the Christian Faith* (Uhrichsville: Barbour and Company, Inc., 1959), 168.

Gloria Patri

188, 196 *Glory be to the Father* . . . This doxology came into being in the early centuries of Christianity; the popular version used here is in public domain, translator unknown.

Gore, Charles

146 *Act for God* . . . Charles Gore, *The Sermon on the Mount: A Practical Exposition* (London: John Murray, Albemarle St. W., 1905), 144.

Grant, Robert

53 *O worship the King* . . . 1833.

Hallesby, Ole

44 *Praise lies upon a higher plane than thanksgiving* . . . Ole Hallesby, *Prayer*, trans. Clarence J. Carlsen (Minneapolis: Augsburg Publishing House, 1994), 143.

166 *Prayer should be the means* . . . Ibid., 38.

Hart, Joseph

61 *Come, ye sinners, poor and needy* . . . 1759.

Havergal, Frances Ridley

56 *Yea, let my whole life be* . . . Frances Havergal, "IV. Adoration," *The Poetical Works of Frances Ridley Havergal* (London: James Nisbet & Co., 1884), 153.

146 *We give thanks* . . . *Golden Thoughts from the Life and Works of Frances Ridley Havergal* (New York: E. P. Dutton and Company, 1892), 53.

Heber, Reginald

40 *Holy, holy, holy!* 1826.

Henry, Matthew

170 *The gracious soul dwells in God* . . . Matthew Henry, *A Method for Prayer* 🍎 (Ross-shire: Christian Focus Publications, 1994), 222.

192 *By morning and evening prayer* . . . Ibid., 168.

195 *Lord, let Thy peace rule in our hearts* . . . Ibid.

Herbert, George

155 *Thou that has given so much to me* . . . George Herbert (1593–1633), "Gratefulness," available on *Bartleby.com*, accessed Sept. 26, 2016, http://www.bartleby.com/371/321.html.

Hugo, Victor

199 *Courage, then, and patience!* Victor Hugo, *The Letters of Victor Hugo from Exile, and after the Fall of the Empire,* Paul Meurice, ed. (Boston and New York: Houghton, Mifflin and Company, 1898), 23.

5, 201 *Good-night! Good-night!* Victor Hugo, "Good-Night," Bertha Hazard, ed., *Three Years with the Poets* (Boston: Houghton Mifflin Co., 1904), 15.

Ingelow, Jean

101 *I have lived to thank God* . . . Clyde Francis Lytle, ed., *Leaves of Gold* (Williamsport: Coslett Publishing Company, 1938), 153.

Keble, John

49 *The trivial round, the common task* . . . John Keble, "New Every Morning Is the Love," 1822.

Ken, Thomas

53 *Praise God, from whom all blessings flow* . . . 1674.

King Jr., Martin Luther

183 *And now unto him who is able* . . . Quoted in Horton Davies, ed., *The Communion of Saints: Prayers of the Famous* (Grand Rapids: William B. Eerdmans Publishing Company, 1990), 16.

Kuyper, Abraham

90 *There is not a square inch in the whole domain* . . . James D. Bratt, ed., *Abraham Kuyper: A Centennial Reader* (Grand Rapids: Wm. B. Eerdmans Publishing Co., 1998), 461.

Law, William

55 *When God has all that He should have* . . . *The Works of the Reverend William Law, M.A.* (London: J. Richardson, 1762), 35.

Leighton, Robert

108 *This is believing indeed . . . The Works of Robert Leighton* (London: W. Nicholson, 1805), 211.

Lemmel, Helen H.

104 *Turn your eyes upon Jesus . . .* 1922.

Lewis, C. S.

11 *To what will you look for help . . . ?* C. S. Lewis, *Mere Christianity* 🍂 (Harper Collins, 1952), 59.

32 *In commanding us to glorify Him . . .* C. S. Lewis, *The Joyful Christian* (New York: Touchstone Publishing, 1977), 120.

54 *We may ignore, but we can nowhere evade . . .* C. S. Lewis, *Letters to Malcolm: Chiefly on Prayer* (San Diego: Harcourt, 1964), 75.

79 *How little people know . . .* C. S. Lewis, *Letter to an American Lady* (Grand Rapids: Wm. B. Eerdmans Publishing Co. 1971), 19.

121 *Christ says, "Give me All."* Lewis, *The Joyful Christian*, 120.

169 *Joy is the serious business of Heaven.* Lewis, *Letters to Malcolm*, 93.

172 *God cannot give us . . .* Lewis, *Mere Christianity*, 50.

Lloyd-Jones, David Martyn

64 *The man who is truly forgiven . . .* Martyn Lloyd-Jones, *Studies in the Sermon on the Mount* (Grand Rapids: Wm. B. Eerdmans Publishing, 1959), 12.

125 *We are walking through this world . . .* David Martyn Lloyd-Jones, *Spiritual Depression* 🍂 (Grand Rapids: Wm. Eerdmans, 1965), 224.

Luther, Martin

71 *We are not yet what we shall be . . .* Martin Luther, *An Argument in Defense of All the Articles of Dr. Martin Luther Wrongly Condemned in the Roman Bull*, available on *GodRules.net*, accessed June 23, 2016, http://www.godrules.net/library/luther/NEW1luther_c4.htm.

92 *In the old days this sound advice was given . . .* Quoted in Roland H. Bainton, *Here I Stand: A Life of Martin Luther* (New York: Abingdon-Cokesbury Press, 1950), 302.

111 *We shall oppose both men and the devil . . .* Quoted in Archie Parrish, *A Simple Way to Pray* 🍂 (Atlanta: Serve International, 2003), 19.

176 *A mighty fortress is our God . . .* 1529, trans. Frederic H. Hedge, 1853.

Lutzer, Erwin W.

88 *Temptation is not a sin* . . . Erwin W. Lutzer, *Getting to No: How to Break a Stubborn Habit* (Colorado Springs: David C. Cook, 2007), 61.

MacArthur, John

40 *It is He who brought us* . . . John MacArthur, *A Year of Prayer* (Eugene: Harvest House Publishers, 2011), Kindle.

180 *You are our light and our salvation* . . . Ibid.

MacDonald, George

51 *My life and death belong to thee* . . . George MacDonald, "A Book of Dreams," *A Hidden Life: And Other Poems* (London: Longman, Green, Longman, Roberts, & Green, 1864), 78.

127 *Thy will be done.* George MacDonald, *Diary of an Old Soul* (London: Mr. Hughes, 1880), 15.

171 *In every gladness, Lord* . . . George MacDonald, *Poems* (London: Longman, Brown, Green, Longmans, & Roberts, 1857), 75.

197 *We are like to Him* . . . George MacDonald, *Annals of a Quiet Neighborhood* (New York: Harper & Brothers, 1867), 135.

Machen, J. Gresham

51 *Christ made the beauty of the world* . . . J. Gresham Machen, "Constraining Love" (transcript), *The Orthodox Presbyterian Church*, accessed Sept. 12, 2016, http://opc.org/machen/ConstrainingLove.html.

214 *Christ's love will do more than restrain us from evil.* Ibid.

Maclaren, Alexander

144 *Seek, as a plain duty* . . . Alexander Maclaren, *Week-day Evening Addresses* (London: Macmillan & Co., 1877), 146.

Maurice, Priscilla

151 *Begin with thanking him for some little thing* . . . Priscilla Maurice, *Sickness, Its Trials and Blessings* (New York: Thomas N. Stanford, 1856), 247.

M'Cheyne, Robert Murray

61 *There is peace with God* . . . *The Sermons of the Rev. Robert Murray McCheyne* (New York: Robert Carter, 1848), 89.

172 *Christ for us is all our righteousness* . . . Attributed to Robert Murray M'Cheyne in a speech by Bishop Handley Moule quoted in Raymond Edman, *They Found the Secret: 20 Transformed Lives That Reveal a Touch of Eternity* 🐝 (Grand Rapids: Zondervan, 1960), 92.

Miller, J. R.

83 *But really the habit of unceasing prayer* . . . J. R. Miller, *Our New Edens* (Philadelphia: Presbyterian Board of Publication and Sabbath-School Work, 1903), 52.

174 *The all-victorious Christ* . . . J. R. Miller, "The Blessing of Cheerfulness," 1895, *GraceGems*, accessed June 23, 2016, http://gracegems.org/Miller/blessing_of_cheerfulness.htm.

Monsell, John S. B.

6, 22 *Christ is the path* . . . John S. B. Monsell, "Fight the Good Fight with All Thy Might," 1863.

Montgomery, James

73 *Nor prayer is made by man alone* . . . James Montgomery, "Prayer Is the Soul's Sincere Desire," 1818.

219 *O Thou by whom we come to God* . . . Ibid.

Mueller, George

112 *Be encouraged, dear Christian reader* . . . *The Autobiography of George Müeller* 🐝 (New Kensington: Whitaker House, 1984), 296.

Murray, Andrew

14 *Just because your heart is cold* . . . Andrew Murray, *With Christ in the School of Prayer: Thoughts on Our Training for the Ministry of Intercession* 🐝 (New York: Fleming H. Revell Company, n.d.), 19.

45 *It is the adoring worship of God* . . . Ibid., 97.

75 *Give us grace to repent every day* . . . Andrew Murray, *A Method for Prayer* (Ross-shire: Christian Focus Publications Ltd., 1994), 171.

101 *Let us each find out what the work is* . . . Murray, *The School of Prayer*, 209–10.

106 *May He give us a large and strong heart* . . . Ibid., ix.

110 *God will not delay one moment longer* . . . Ibid., 120.

Patrick of Ireland

42 *I bind unto myself today* . . . "St. Patrick's Breastplate," attributed to Patrick of Ireland (372–466), trans. Cecil Frances Alexander, 1889.

5, 202 *Christ be beside me* . . . "Christ Be Beside Me," © 1969 James Quinn. Published by OCP. All rights reserved. Used with permission. This is an adaptation of "St. Patrick's Breastplate," attributed to Patrick of Ireland.

Peace Prayer

109 *Lord, make me an instrument of Thy peace* . . . This prayer is commonly attributed to Francis of Assisi but was likely written in the early 1900s. This translation from the French is assumed to be in public domain.

Piper, John

20 *Until you believe that life is war* . . . John Piper, "Prayer: The Work of Missions" (transcript), *desiringGod*, July 29, 1988, accessed June 22, 2016, http://www.desiringgod.org/messages/prayer-the-work-of-missions.

41 *God is most glorified in us* . . . John Piper, *Desiring God: Meditations of a Christian Hedonist* 🍂 (Colorado Springs: Multnomah, 1986), 309.

62 *What is sin?* John Piper, "What Is Sin? The Essence and Root of All Sinning" (transcript), *desiringGod*, Feb. 2, 2015, accessed Sept. 3, 2016, http://www.desiringgod.org/messages/the-origin-essence-and -definition-of-sin.

120 *The strength of patience hangs* . . . John Piper, *Battling Unbelief: Defeating Sin with Superior Pleasure* 🍂 (Colorado Springs: Mult-nomah Books, 2007), 75.

152 *Thanksgiving stirreth up thankfulness* . . . John Piper, *When the Dark-ness Will Not Lift* (Wheaton: Crossway, 2006), 51.

189 *Christ has said "Amen" to us.* John Piper, "Amen: A Word Common to Many Languages" (transcript), *desiringGod*, February 1, 1998, accessed Sept. 26, 2016, http://www.desiringgod.org/resource-library /sermons/amen.

Prentiss, Elizabeth

18 *Let people pray* . . . George Lewis Prentiss, *More Love to Thee: The Life and Letters of Elizabeth Prentiss* 🍂 (Amityville: Calvary Press, 1994), 55.

74 *Say over and over to yourself* . . . Elizabeth Prentiss, *Stepping Heaven-ward* 🍂 (Waverly: Lamplighter Publishing, 1997), 50.

85 *Oh, you don't know what a great sinner I am* . . . Prentiss, *More Love to Thee*, 97.

127 *Doubt everything* . . . Prentiss, *Stepping Heavenward*, 339.

137 *We only know ourselves and what we really are* . . . Ibid., 168.

139 *The light affliction is nothing* . . . Prentiss, *More Love to Thee*, 253.

Rinkart, Martin

158 *Now thank we all our God* . . . 1636, trans. Catherine Winkworth, 1856.

159 *All praise and thanks to God* . . . Ibid., 1856.

Robertson, Frederick W.

87 *To get up every morning with the firm resolve* . . . Frederick W. Robertson, *The Human Race and Other Sermons* (London: C. Kegan Paul & Co., 1880), 33.

Rossetti, Christina

131 *O Lord, who art our Guide even unto death* . . . Mary W. Tileston, ed., *Daily Strength for Daily Needs* ❦ (Cambridge: University Press, 1884), 23.

182 *O Lord, Our Refuge from the storm* . . . Mary Wilder Tileston, ed., *Prayers Ancient and Modern* (New York: Grosset & Dunlap, 1928), 55.

Rutherford, Samuel

62 *Hurt not your conscience* . . . *Letters of the Reverend Samuel Rutherford* (Edinburgh: Duncan Grant, 1867), 95.

Ryle, J. C.

16 *In every journey* . . . J. C. Ryle, *A Call to Prayer* ❦ (Laurel, MS: Audubon Press, n.d.), 26.

23 *Praying and sinning will never live together* . . . Ibid., 15.

Schaeffer, Edith

56 *If we were trying to fill up a silver cup of reverence* . . . Edith Schaeffer, *The Life of Prayer* (Wheaton: Crossway, 1992), 133.

Sproul, R.C.

196 *To live* coram Deo *is to* . . . R.C. Sproul, "What Does 'Coram Deo' Mean?" *Ligonier Ministries*, accessed Sept. 12, 2016, http://www.ligonier.org/blog/what-does-coram-deo-mean/.

Spurgeon, Charles Haddon

19 *I always feel it well . . .* Quoted in Steve J. Miller, *C. H. Spurgeon on Spiritual Leadership* (Chicago: Moody, 2003), 14.

43 *Praise is the rehearsal . . .* Charles Haddon Spurgeon, *Metropolitan Tabernacle Pulpit*, Vol XXXVI (London: Passmore & Alabaster, 1890), 12.

100 *I will help you.* Charles Haddon Spurgeon, *Morning by Morning* (Grand Rapids: Zondervan, 2008), 16.

107 *Earnest intercession will be sure to bring love with it.* Charles Haddon Spurgeon, *Metropolitan Tabernacle Pulpit*, Vol. XVIII (London: Passmore & Alabaster, 1872), 258.

146 *The Lord continues to bless . . .* Charles Haddon Spurgeon "Knowledge. Worship. Gratitude" (sermon no. 1763), *The Spurgeon Archive*, accessed August 11, 2016, http://www.romans45.org/spurgeon/sermons/1763 .htm.

146 *Thankless rebels!* Ibid.

147 *You that are saved . . .* Ibid.

149 *When you glorify God as God . . .* Ibid.

152 *Let us even at this present moment . . .* C. H. Spurgeon, *The Treasury of David*, Vol. 5, (New York: Funk & Wagnalls, 1882), 320.

Stowe, Harriet Beecher

210 *Are there any bound to us . . . ?* Harriet Beecher Stowe, *Religious Studies, Sketches and Poems* (Cambridge: Riverside Press, 1896), 149.

Taylor, Helen L.

181 *If you are one of the King's pilgrims . . .* Helen L. Taylor, *Little Pilgrim's Progress: From John Bunyan's Classic* ❦ (Chicago: Moody, 2013), 24.

Taylor, Hudson

122 *Difficulties afford a platform . . .* Quoted in Dr. and Mrs. Howard Taylor, *Hudson Taylor's Spiritual Secret* ▨ (Chicago: Moody Press, 1989), 186.

165 *Our joy in Him may be a fluctuating thing . . .* J. Hudson Taylor, "Strength for Service," *China's Millions* 6, no. 67 (1881): 146.

Taylor, Jeremy

124 *Enjoy the blessings of this day . . .* Jeremy Taylor, *The Rules and Exercises of Holy Living and Dying* (London: J. G. & F. Rivington, 1838), 102.

Trench, Richard Chenevix

Trumbull, Charles G.

Upham, Thomas C.

Valley of Vision, The ❦